INTRODUCTION

> **des•per•ate** (des'-pə-rət, -prət) adj. **1:** reckless or dangerous because of despair or urgency: a desperate criminal. **2:** having an urgent need, desire, etc.: desperate to get attention. **3:** extremely intense; intolerable or shocking: clothes in desperate taste.

You may be wondering just what makes this a book of "desperate" knitting.

First, we've chosen designs that use some of the lushest yarns out there, thus filling our "desperate" desire to buy and wear yarns that are oh, so touchable.

Second, our designers have kept the techniques at a stress-free level because we are "desperate" to get rid of any extra annoyance or frustration. We have chosen knitting partly for its Zen qualities. After all, knitting is considered the "new yoga."

Third, the silhouettes and styling details make it clear that we enjoy being women and, depending on how we accessorize and wear them, some may say they are in "desperate" taste.

Of course, you must have the right party as a means to our "desperate" ends, so we have included projects for entertaining and socializing that reflect the inner knitter!

TABLE OF CONTENTS

Favorite Daydream 4
Juice It Up 6
Off-the-Shoulder Sweater 9
Foxy Lady 11
Strut Your Stuff 15
Afternoon Delight 17
Shopping Spree Cardigan 19
Shopping Spree Tank 22
Impress the Board 24
Added Spice Scarf 28
Green-With-Envy Scarf 30
Flower Pins 32
Carmen Shoulder Bag 34

American School of Needlework, Berne, IN 46711 • ASNpub.com

Zingy Zebra Purse   35
Bring On the Bling   37
Charitable-Event Ponchette   40
Ruffled Romance   42
Work-It-Out Warmers   45
Yoga Mat   47
Evening Interlude   48
BYOB Bag   50
Potluck Performers   52
Potluck Hostess   54
Let's Get Together   56
Knitting Basics   59

American School of Needlework, Berne, IN 46711 • ASNpub.com

FAVORITE DAYDREAM

Design by Scarlet Taylor

Skill Level

EASY

Sizes

Woman's extra-small (small, medium, large) Instructions are given for smallest size, with larger sizes in parentheses. When only 1 number is given, it applies to all sizes.

Finished Measurements

Bust: 32½ (35, 38½, 43) inches
Length (front, without straps): 16 (16½, 17½, 18½) inches

Materials

Bulky weight yarn (4 oz/140 yds/113g per skein): 2 (2, 3, 4) skeins preppie #3427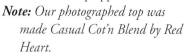

Note: Our photographed top was made Casual Cot'n Blend by Red Heart.

Size 10 (6mm) knitting needles or size needed to obtain gauge
Size 10 (6mm) double-pointed needles for I-Cord
Stitch holders

Gauge

14 sts and 19 rows = 4 inches/10cm in St st
To save time, take time to check gauge.

Special Abbreviations

Slip, slip, knit (ssk): Sl next 2 sts knitwise one at a time from left to right needle, insert LH needle through fronts of these sts and k2tog to dec 1 st.

Make 1 (M1): Inc 1 by inserting LH needle under horizontal thread between st just worked and next st, knit through the back lp.

Purl 2 together through back loops (p2tog-tbl): Purl next 2 sts tog through their back lps.

Pattern Notes

To work fully fashioned dec for armholes:
RS rows: K1, ssk, work to last 3 sts, k2tog, k1.
WS rows: P1, p2tog, work to last 3 sts, p2tog-tbl, p1.

To work fully fashioned dec for front neck shaping:
RS rows: Work across first side in pat until 3 sts rem, k2tog, k1; on 2nd side, k1, ssk, work in pat across.
WS rows: Work across first side in pat until 3 sts rem, p2tog-tbl, p1; on 2nd side, p1, p2tog work in pat across.

Back

Cast on 49 (53, 59, 67) sts.

Purl 1 row.

Work in St st until piece measures approx 2 (2, 3, 3) inches from beg, ending with a WS row.

Next row (RS): K2, M1, knit to last 2 sts, M1, k2. (51, 55, 61, 69 sts)

Continue in St st working inc row as above every 8th (8th, 8th, 10th) row 3 times more. (57, 61, 67, 75 sts)

Work even in St st until piece measures approx 11½ (12, 12½, 13) inches from beg, ending with a WS row.

Armhole shaping

Bind off 4 (4, 5, 5) sts at beg of next 2 rows, 3 sts at beg of next 2 rows, 0 (0, 0, 2) sts at beg of next 2 rows, then work fully fashioned dec each side every row 8 (9, 10, 11) times. (27, 29, 31, 33 sts)

Work even, if necessary, until piece measures approx 14 (15, 15½, 16½) inches from beg, ending with a RS row.

Neck shaping

Row 1 (WS): P3, knit to last 3 sts, p3.

Row 2 (RS): K3, place these sts on holder; bind off next 21 (23, 25, 27) sts, knit rem sts.

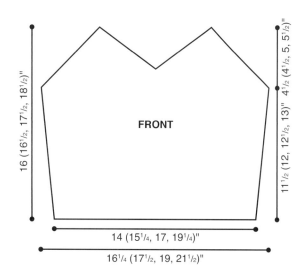

16 (16½, 17½, 18½)"

11½ (12, 12½, 13)"

4½ (4½, 5, 5½)"

FRONT

14 (15¼, 17, 19¼)"

16¼ (17½, 19, 21½)"

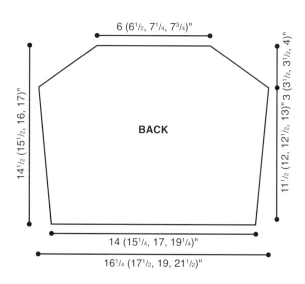

6 (6½, 7¼, 7¾)"

14½ (15½, 16, 17)"

11½ (12, 12½, 13)"

3 (3½, 3½, 4)"

BACK

14 (15¼, 17, 19¼)"

16¼ (17½, 19, 21½)"

American School of Needlework, Berne, IN 46711 • ASNpub.com

I-cord straps

Sl rem 3 sts onto dpn; working on RS, *k3, slide sts to end of needle; rep from * until I-cord measures 12 inches, place sts on holder.

Place 3 sts from holder onto dpn and rep for other strap.

Front

Work same as for back to armhole.

Armhole shaping

Bind off 4 (4, 5, 5) sts at beg of next 2 rows, 3 sts at beg of next 2 rows, then 0 (0, 0, 2) sts at beg of next 2 rows. (43, 47 51, 55 sts)

Continue to shape armhole, working fully fashioned dec each side this row, and [every other row] 7 (8, 9, 10) times and *at the same time* shape neck as follows:

Neck shaping

Work across first 19 (21, 23, 25) sts, k2tog; join 2nd skein of yarn and bind off next st; ssk, work across rem sts. (20, 22, 24, 26 sts on each side)

Working both sides at once with separate skeins of yarn, work 1 row even.

Work fully fashioned dec each neck edge [every row] 2 (3, 3, 5) times, then [every other row] 6 (6, 7, 6) times. (4 sts on each side)

Next row (WS): P1, p2tog, p1.

Work I-cord on rem 3 sts on each side, for approx 11 inches. Place sts on holder.

Finishing

Sew side seams. Tie I-cord straps and check for desired length, adjust if necessary and bind off.

JUICE IT UP

Design by Scarlet Taylor

Skill Level

INTERMEDIATE

Size

Woman's small (medium, large, extra-large) Instructions are given for smallest size, with larger sizes in parentheses. When only 1 number is given, it applies to all sizes.

Finished Measurements

Chest: 32½ (36, 40, 44) inches
Length: 19½ (20½, 21, 22) inches

Materials

Worsted weight yarn (3.5 oz/ 186 yds/100g per skein): 4 (5, 6, 6) skeins tangerine #3252

MEDIUM

Note: Our photographed sweater was made with TLC Cotton Plus.
Size 8 (5mm) knitting needles or size needed to obtain gauge
Stitch holders

Gauge

21 sts and 28 rows = 4 inches/10cm in rib pat, slightly stretched
To save time, take time to check gauge.

Special Abbreviations

Slip, slip, knit (ssk): Slip next 2 sts knitwise one at a time from left to right needle, insert LH needle through fronts of these sts and k2tog to dec 1 st.
Make 1 (M1): Inc 1 by inserting LH needle under horizontal thread between st just worked and next st, knit through the back lp.

Back

Cast on 79 (89, 99, 109) sts.

Row 1 (RS): K2, *p2, sl 1 wyib, p2, k2, sl 1 wyib, k2; rep from * to last 7 sts; p2, sl 1 wyib, p2, k2.

Row 2 (WS): P2, *k2, p1, k2, p5; rep from * to last 7 sts, k2, p1, k2, p2.

Rep Rows 1 and 2 until piece measures approx 3 inches from beg, ending with a WS row.

Inc row (RS): K1, M1, work in pat to last st, M1, k1.

Continue in pat as established inc as before, [every 18th row] once, then [every 20th row] once working extra sts into pat. (85, 95, 105, 115 sts)

Continue even in pat until piece measures approx 10½ (11, 11, 11½) inches from beg, ending with a WS row.

Armhole shaping

Bind off 2 sts at beg of next 2 rows, then 0 (0, 0, 2) sts at beg of next 2 rows.

Continue in pat dec 1 st each side by k1, ssk, work to last 3 sts, k2tog, k1 [every other row] 2 (6, 6, 6) times. (77, 79, 89, 95 sts)

Work even in pat as established until piece measures approx 18½ (19½, 20, 21) inches, ending with a WS row, dec 1 st across last row. (76, 78, 88, 94 sts)

Shoulder shaping

Bind off 7 (7, 9, 9) sts at beg of next 4 rows, then 7 (8, 8, 9) sts at beg of next 2 rows.

Bind off rem 34 (34, 36, 40) sts for back neck.

Front

Work same as for Back to Armhole shaping.

Neck & armhole shaping

Shape armholes same as for back and *at the same time* when armhole measures approx 1½ (2, 2, 2½) inches shape neck as follows:

Next row (RS): Work in pat across first 38 (39, 44, 47) sts; join 2nd skein of yarn and bind off center st, work rem sts in pat.

Note: Work both sides at once with separate skeins of yarn.

Next row: Work in pat across.

Next row (dec row): Work in pat across first shoulder to last 5 sts, k2tog, p1, k1, p1; on 2nd shoulder, p1, k1, p1, ssk, work in pat across.

Next row: Work in pat across first shoulder to last 5 sts, p2, k1, p1, k1; on 2nd shoulder, k1, p1, k1, p2, work in pat across.

Continue in pat dec on next and [every other row] 4 (4, 4, 8) times, then [every 4th row] 8 (8, 9, 7) times. (24, 25, 29, 30 sts on each shoulder)

Continue even, if necessary, until piece measures same as back to shoulder, ending with a WS Row.

Shoulder shaping

Bind off 7 (7, 9, 9) sts at beg of next 4 rows, then 7 (8, 8, 9) sts at beg of next 2 row. (3 sts on each shoulder)

Place sts on holders for neck band rib.

Sleeves

Make 2

Cast on 50 (50, 60, 60) sts.

Row 1 (RS): K3, *p2, sl 1 wyib, p2, k2, sl 1 wyib, k2; rep from * to last 7 sts, p2, sl 1 wyib, p2, k2.

Row 2 (WS): P2, *k2, p1, k2, p5; rep from * to last 8 sts, k2, p1, k2, p3.

Rep Rows 1 and 2 inc 1 st by M1 each side [every other row] 6 (10, 12, 16) times, then [every 4th row] 9 (7, 6, 4) times. (80, 84, 96, 100 sts)

Work even in pat until piece measures approx 8 (7½, 7½, 7¾) inches, ending with a WS row.

Bind off 2 sts at beg of next 2 rows, then 0 (0, 0, 2) sts at beg of next 2 rows.

Continue in pat dec 1 st each side by k1, ssk, work to last 3 sts, k2tog, k1 [every other row] 2 (6, 6, 6) times. (72, 68, 80, 80 sts)

Work 1 row even.

Bind off all sts.

Assembly
Sew shoulder seams.

Neck band
Continue rib pat as established over rem 3 sts on each shoulder until pieces, when slightly stretched, meet at center back of neck.

Bind off.

Finishing
Sew edges of neck band ribs to neckline then sew bound-off edges tog. Set in sleeves. Sew sleeve and side seams. Weave in all ends.

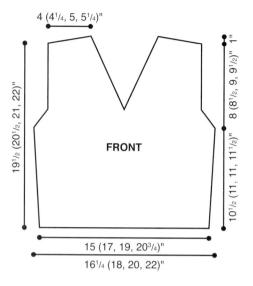

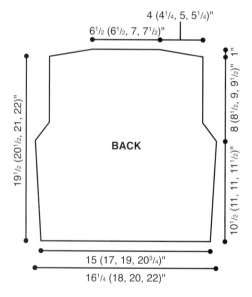

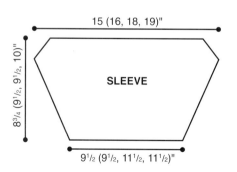

OFF-THE-SHOULDER SWEATER

Design by Svetlana Avrakh

Skill Level

EASY

Sizes

Woman's small (medium, large, extra-large) Instructions are given for smallest size, with larger sizes in parentheses. When only 1 number is given, it applies to all sizes.

Finished Measurements

Chest: 37 (42, 45, 49) inches

Materials

Bulky weight yarn (3.5 oz/ 142 yds/100g per ball): 3 (4, 4) balls each icicle white #06006 (A) and soft earth #06011 (B)

Note: Our photographed sweater was made with Patons Divine

Size 15 (10mm) knitting needles or size needed to obtain gauge

Gauge

8 sts and 10 rows = 4 inches/10cm in St st with 1 strand each of A and B held tog
To save time, take time to check gauge.

Special Abbreviation

Purl 2 together through back loops (p2tog-tbl): Purl next 2 sts tog through their back lps.

Pattern Note

Sweater is worked with 1 strand of A and B held tog throughout.

Back/Front

Make 2

With 1 strand of each A and B held tog, cast on 36 (42, 46, 50) sts.

For sizes small, medium and extra-large only

Row 1 (RS): K4 (3, 3), *p4, k4; rep from * to last 0 (7, 7) sts, [p4, k3] 0 (1, 1) time.

Row 2: [P3, k4] 0 (1, 1) time, *p4, k4; rep from * to last 4 (3, 3) sts, p4 (3, 3).

Continue with For All Sizes below.

For size large only

Row 1 (RS): P1, *k4, p4; rep from * to last 5 sts, k4, p1.

Row 2: K1, p4, *k4, p4; rep from * to last st, k1.

Continue with For All Sizes.

For All Sizes

Rep Rows 1 and 2 until work measures 12 inches from beg ending with WS row.

Raglan shaping

Continuing in pat, bind off 3 (3, 4, 4) sts beg next 2 rows. (30, 36, 38, 42 sts)

Row 1 (RS): K2, k2tog, work in pat to last 4 sts, sl 1k, k1, psso, k2.

Row 2: P2, p2tog-tbl, work in pat to last 4 sts, p2tog, p2.

[Rep Rows 1 and 2] 0 (1, 1, 1) time more. (26, 28, 30, 34 sts)

Next row: K2, k2tog, work in pat to last 4 sts, sl 1k, k1, psso, k2.

Next row: Knit all knit sts and purl all purl sts as they appear.

Rep last 2 rows 3 (3, 3, 4) times more.

Bind off rem 18 (20, 22, 24) sts.

Sleeves

With 1 strand of A and B held tog, cast on 20 sts.

Row 1 (RS): K4, *p4, k4; rep from * across.

Row 2: P4, *k4, p4; rep from * across.

Rep Rows 1 and 2, inc 1 st each end of needle [every 7th row] once, then [every 6th row] 2 (3, 4, 4) times working inc sts into pat. (26, 28, 30, 30 sts)

Continue even in established pat until sleeve measures 17½ (18½, 18½, 19) inches from beg, ending with WS row.

Raglan shaping

Continuing in pat, bind off 3 (3, 4, 4) sts at beg next 2 rows. (20, 22, 22, 22 sts)

Row 1 (RS): K2, k2tog, work in pat to last 4 sts, sl 1k, k1, psso, k2.

Row 2: P2, p2tog-tbl, work in pat to last 4 sts, p2tog, p2. (16, 18, 18, 18 sts)

Next row: K2, k2tog, work in pat to last 4 sts, sl 1k, k1, psso, k2.

Next row: Knit all knit sts and purl all purl sts as they appear.

[Rep last 2 rows] 3 (4, 3, 4) times more.

Bind off rem 8 sts.

Assembly

Sew raglan seams.

Collar

With 1 strand each of A and B held tog, cast on 29 sts.

Row 1 (RS): K1, *p1, k1; rep from * across.

Row 2: P1, *k1, p1; rep from * across.

Rep Rows 1 and 2 until collar, without stretching, fits around neck edge.

Finishing

Sew collar to neck edge, beg at center of back. Sew side and sleeve seams.

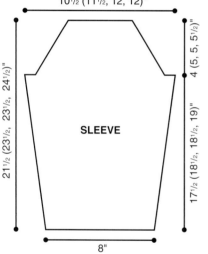

9 (10, 11, 12)"

16 (17, 17, 17½)"

FRONT & BACK

4 (5, 5, 5½)"

12"

18½ (21, 22½, 24½)"

10½ (11½, 12, 12)"

21½ (23½, 23½, 24½)"

SLEEVE

4 (5, 5, 5½)"

17½ (18½, 18½, 19)"

8"

FOXY LADY

Design by Darla Sims

Skill Level

EASY

Sizes

Woman's small (medium, large, extra-large) Instructions are given for smallest size, with larger sizes in parentheses. When only 1 number is given, it applies to all sizes.

Finished Measurements

Chest: 40 (44, 48, 52) inches

Materials

Worsted weight yarn (1.75oz/98 yds/50g per ball): 7 (7, 8, 9) balls pecan #3664 (MC)

Worsted weight novelty yarn (1.76 oz/ 87 yds/50g per ball): 2 (2, 2, 3) balls Sahara #9935 (CC)

Note: *Our photographed sweater was made with Mode Dea Dream and Mode Dea Chichi.*

Size 7 (4.5mm) knitting needles
Size 10 (6mm) straight and circular knitting needles or size needed to obtain gauge
2 yds ⅝-inch-wide black velvet ribbon
Sewing needle and matching thread

Gauge

8 sts and 9 rows = 2 inches/5cm in St st with larger needles
To save time, take time to check gauge.

Back

With larger straight needles and MC, cast on 80 (88, 96, 104) sts.

Beg with knit row as RS, work 4 rows even in St st.

Continuing in St st, dec 1 st by k1, k2tog, knit to last 3 sts, ssk, k1, each end [every 6th row] 5 times. (70, 78, 86, 94 sts)

Work 4 rows even in St st.

Inc 1 st, each end [every 4th row] 5 times. (80, 88, 96, 104 sts)

Work even in St st until piece measures 13½ inches.

Armhole shaping

Bind off 10 (12, 13, 15) sts at the beg of next 2 rows. (60, 64, 70, 74 sts)

Next row (dec row): K1, k2tog, knit to last 3 sts, ssk, k1. (58, 62, 68, 72 sts)

Dec 1 st each end [every other row] twice more. (54, 58, 64, 68 sts)

Work even in St st until armhole measures 9 (9½, 10, 10½).

Shoulder shaping

Bind off 5 (5, 5, 6) sts at the beg of next 4 rows. (34, 38, 44, 44 sts)

Bind off 6 (6, 7, 7) sts at the beg of next 2 rows. (22, 26, 30, 30 sts)

Bind off rem sts.

Right Front

With larger straight needles and MC, cast on 4 (8, 12, 16) sts.

Row 1 (RS): Knit.

Row 2: Purl.

Front edge shaping

Continue in St st, cast on 4 sts at front edge only, [every RS row] twice, cast on 3 sts [every RS row] 3 times, cast on 2 sts [every RS row] 6 times, cast on 1 st [every RS row] 7 (6, 5, 5) times.

Work 14 rows even.

Dec 1 st at neck edge only on next RS row.

Dec 1 st at neck edge only [every 4th row] 10 (11, 12, 12) times.

At the same time:

Side shaping

For side edge, work 2 rows, then dec 1 st at side edge only [every 6th row] 5 times, work 4 rows even, then inc 1 st at side edge only [every 4th row] 5 times.

Work until piece is same length same as back to underarm.

Armhole shaping

Note: *Continue center front shaping as above while working armhole shaping.*

Bind off 10 (12, 13, 15) sts at the beg of next row. Dec 1 st armhole edge only [every RS row] 3 times.

Work even in St st until armhole measures 9 (9½, 10, 10½) ending by working a RS row.

Shoulder shaping

Row 1 (WS): Bind off 5 (5, 5, 6) sts, purl across.

Row 2: Knit.

Rows 3 and 4: Rep Rows 1 and 2.

Bind off rem 6 (6, 7, 7) sts.

Left Front

With larger straight needles and MC, cast on 4 (8, 12, 16) sts.

Row 1 (RS): Knit.

Row 2: Purl.

Front edge shaping

Work in St st, cast on 4 sts, at front edge only, [every RS row] twice, cast on 3

sts [every RS row] 3 times, cast on 2 sts [every RS row] 6 times, cast on 1 st [every RS row] 7 (6, 5, 5) times.

Work 14 rows even.

Dec 1 st at neck edge only on next RS row.

Dec 1 st at neck edge only [every 4th row] 10 (11, 12, 12) times.

At the same time:

Side shaping

For side edge, work 2 rows, then dec 1 st at side edge only [every 6th row] 5 times, work 4 rows even, then inc 1 st at side edge only [every 4th row] 5 times.

Work until piece is same length same as back to underarm, ending by working a WS row.

Armhole shaping

Note: *Continue center front shaping as above while working armhole shaping.*

Bind off 10 (12, 13, 15) sts at the beg of next row. Dec 1 st armhole edge only [every RS row] 3 times.

Work even in St st until armhole measures 9 (9½, 10, 10½) ending by working a WS row

Shoulder shaping

Row 1 (RS): Bind off 5 (5, 5, 6) sts, knit across.

Row 2: Purl.

Rows 3 and 4: Rep Rows 1 and 2.

Bind off rem 6 (6, 7, 7) sts.

Sleeves

With larger straight needles cast on 40 (42, 44, 46) sts.

Work 4 rows in St st.

Change to smaller needles.

Work 6 rows in k1, p1 rib.

Change to larger needles.

Work in St st, inc 1 st each end [every 6th row] 12 times. (60, 62, 64, 66 sts)

Work even until sleeve measures 15½ inches.

Sleeve cap shaping

Bind off 10 (12, 13, 15) sts at the beg of next 2 rows. (40, 38, 38, 36 sts)

Dec 1 st each end [every other row] 3 times. (34, 32, 32, 30 sts)

Work 10 (12, 14, 16) rows even.

Dec 1 st each end [every row] 10 times. (14, 12, 12, 10 sts)

Bind off all sts.

Assembly

Sew shoulder seams.

Sleeve edging

With larger needles and CC, with RS facing, pick and knit in each st across lower edge of sleeve. Work 5 rows in garter st.

Bind off all sts.

Finishing

Sew in sleeves, matching center of sleeve to shoulder seam. Sew side and sleeve in one continuous seam.

Outer edging

With circular needle and CC, beg at center back neck, pick and knit 10 sts (11, 11, 13) across back to left shoulder, pick up and knit 84 sts (86, 88, 90) along left front between shoulder seam and side seam, pick up and knit 78 sts (86, 94, 102) sts across lower back edge, pick up and knit 84 (86, 88, 90) sts along right front edge from side seam to right shoulder seam, pick up and knit 10 (11, 12, 13) sts to center back neck. Do not join. Working back and forth in rows, work 9 rows in garter st.

Bind off all sts.

Ribbon trim

Cut 2 (29-inch) lengths of ribbon for sleeves. Placing ribbon above ribbing, with sewing needle and matching thread

tack center of each piece of ribbon to sleeve seam. Tie ends in bow.

Cut rem ribbon in half, referring to photo for placement, sew to fronts of jacket. Tie ends in bows.

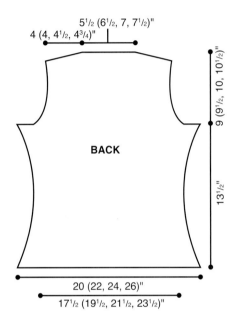

5$\frac{1}{2}$ (6$\frac{1}{2}$, 7, 7$\frac{1}{2}$)"

4 (4, 4$\frac{1}{2}$, 4$\frac{3}{4}$)"

9 (9$\frac{1}{2}$, 10, 10$\frac{1}{2}$)"

BACK

13$\frac{1}{2}$"

20 (22, 24, 26)"

17$\frac{1}{2}$ (19$\frac{1}{2}$, 21$\frac{1}{2}$, 23$\frac{1}{2}$)"

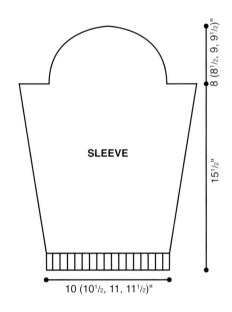

8 (8$\frac{1}{2}$, 9, 9$\frac{1}{2}$)"

SLEEVE

15$\frac{1}{2}$"

10 (10$\frac{1}{2}$, 11, 11$\frac{1}{2}$)"

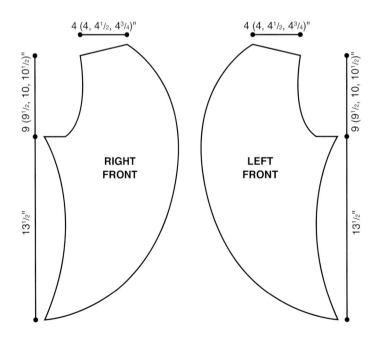

4 (4, 4$\frac{1}{2}$, 4$\frac{3}{4}$)"

4 (4, 4$\frac{1}{2}$, 4$\frac{3}{4}$)"

9 (9$\frac{1}{2}$, 10, 10$\frac{1}{2}$)"

9 (9$\frac{1}{2}$, 10, 10$\frac{1}{2}$)"

RIGHT FRONT

LEFT FRONT

13$\frac{1}{2}$"

13$\frac{1}{2}$"

STRUT YOUR STUFF
Design by Lorna Miser

Skill Level

EASY

Sizes

Woman's extra-small (small, medium, large) Instructions are given for the smallest size, with larger sizes in parentheses. When only 1 number is given, it applies to all sizes.

Finished Measurements

Chest: 30 (34, 38, 42) inches
Length: 17 (18, 19, 20) inches

Materials

Bulky weight yarn (2.5 oz/100 yds/70g per skein): 3 (4, 4, 5) balls moonstone #0002

Note: Our photographed tank top was made with Caron Jewel Box.
Size 7 (4.5mm) knitting needles or size needed to obtain gauge
Matching elastic thread (optional)

Gauge

14 sts = 4 inches in St st
To save time, take time to check gauge.

Special Abbreviation

Slip, slip, knit (ssk): Sl next 2 sts knitwise one at a time from left to right needle, insert LH needle through fronts of these sts and k2tog to dec 1 st.

Back

Cast on 54 (58, 66, 74) sts.

Row 1 (RS): K2, *p2, k2; rep from * across.

Row 2 (WS): P2, *k2, p2; rep from * across. Rep Rows 1 and 2 until piece measures 10 (11, 12, 13) inches from beg.

Armhole shaping

Bind off 2 (3, 3, 5) sts at beg of next 2 rows.

Next row (RS): K2, ssk, work in pat to last 3 sts, k2tog, k2.

Next row (WS): Work in pat across.

Rep last 2 rows 0 (0, 1, 3) times. (48, 50, 56, 56 sts)

Work even in pat until armhole measures 5 (5½, 6, 6 ½) inches.

Neck shaping

Work in pat across 10 (10, 14, 14) sts, join 2nd skein of yarn and bind off center 28 (30, 28, 28) sts, work in pat across rem sts.

Work in pat on both sides at the same time with separate skeins of yarn until armhole measures 7 (7½, 8, 8½) inches.

Bind off all sts.

Front

Work same as for back until armhole measures 3½ (4, 4½, 5) inches.

Neck shaping

Work in pat across 10 (10, 14, 14) sts, join 2nd skein of yarn and bind off center 28 (30, 28, 28) sts, work in pat across rem sts.

Work in pat on both sides at the same time with separate skeins of yarn until armhole measures same length as back.

Bind off all sts.

Finishing

Sew shoulders to back. Sew side seams.

Optional: For a more fitted look weave elastic thread through the lower 4 inches of the tank top on the inside ribbing.

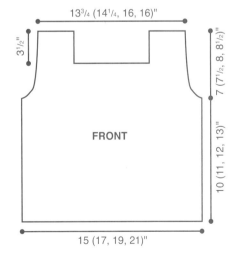

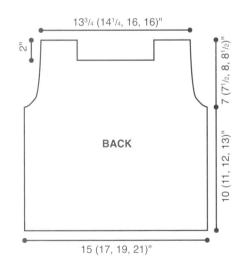

AFTERNOON DELIGHT

Design by Lorna Miser

Skill Level

EASY

Size

Woman's extra-small (small, medium, large) Instructions are given for smallest size, with larger sizes in parentheses. When only 1 number is given, it applies to all sizes.

Finished Measurements

Chest: 32 (36, 40, 44) inches
Length: 13½ (14½, 15½, 16½) inches

Materials

Worsted weight yarn (3.5 oz/186 yds/100g per ball): 2 (3, 3, 4) balls light rose #3706

Note: *Our photographed top was made with TLC Cotton Plus.*

Size 5 (3.75mm) 24-inch circular needles
1 yd twisted satin cord
¼-inch wide elastic (optional)

Gauge

20 sts = 4 inches/10cm in k2, p2 ribbing slightly stretched

Pattern Note

Top is worked in one piece.

Back/Front

Cast on 152 (172, 192, 212) sts. Join, being careful that sts do not twist. Place marker for beg of round.

Rnd 1: *P2, k2; rep from * around.

Rep Rnd 1 until piece measures 11 (12, 13, 14) inches from beg or until 2½ inches shorter than desired length.

Next rnd (eyelet rnd): [P2, k2] 18 (22, 24, 26) times; yo, p2tog, k2, p2tog, yo, k2, [p2, k2] around.

Next 3 rnds: Work even in k2, p2 ribbing.

Rep last 4 rnds 3 times more. (4 eyelet rnds)

Picot bind off

Bind off 2 sts, *sl lp from right needle back to left needle, cast on 2 sts on left

needle, bind off these 2 sts and next 4 sts; rep from * around.

Finishing

Weave twisted satin cord through eyelets. Tie and adjust length of cords. Tie overhand knot in each end and trim.

Optional elastic: To help tube top stay in place more comfortably, cut a piece of elastic about 4 inches shorter than chest measurement where top is worn. Overlap ends of elastic by ½ inch and sew securely tog with thread and needle. Use yarn to embroider cross-sts over but not through the elastic all the way around the top edge. Secure ends.

SHOPPING SPREE CARDIGAN
Design by Scarlet Taylor

Skill Level

EASY

Size
Woman's small (medium, large, extra-large, 2X-large) Instructions are given for smallest size, with larger sizes in parentheses. When only 1 number is given, it applies to all sizes.

Finished Measurements
Chest: 34½ (38½, 42½, 47, 52) inches
Length: 22 (22½, 23, 23½, 24) inches

Materials
Worsted weight yarn (3.5 oz/186 yards/100g per skein): 6 (7, 8, 8, 9) skeins salsa #3270 (A), 1 skein gold #3215 (B)

Note: Our photographed cardigan was made with TLC Cotton Plus.
Size 7 (4.5mm) knitting needles
Size 8 (5mm) knitting needles or size needed to obtain gauge
Stitch holder
10 (⅝-inch) decorative buttons

Gauge
20 sts and 25 rows = 4 inches/10cm in St st with larger needles
To save time, take time to check gauge.

Special Abbreviations
Slip, slip knit (ssk): Sl next 2 sts knitwise one at a time from left to right needle, insert LH needle through fronts of these sts and k2 tog to dec 1 st.

Make 1 (M1): Inc 1 by inserting LH needle under horizontal thread between st just worked and next st, knit through the back lp.

Back
With smaller needles and B cast on 86 (96, 106, 118, 130) sts. Fasten off B.

With A, work in K1, p1 rib for approx 2 inches, ending with a WS row.

Change to larger needles.

Beg St st and work even until piece measures approx 14 inches from beg, ending with a WS row.

Armhole shaping
Bind off 2 (4, 4, 4, 4) sts at beg of next 2 rows, then 0 (2, 0, 2, 2) sts at beg of next 2 rows.

Dec row (RS): K1, ssk, work to last 3 sts, k2tog, k1.

Rep dec row [every other row] 3 (4, 4, 6, 7) times. (74, 74, 88, 92, 102 sts)

Work even in St st until piece measures approx 22 (22 ½, 23, 23 ½, 24) inches from beg, ending with a WS row.

Shoulder shaping
Bind off 20 (19, 25, 27, 32) sts at beg of next 2 rows.

Sl rem 34 (36, 38, 38, 38) sts to st holder for back neck.

Left Front
With smaller needles and B cast on 43 (48, 53, 59, 65) sts. Fasten off B.

With A work in k1, p1 rib for approx 2 inches, ending with a WS row.

Change to larger needles.

Work even in St st until piece measures approx 14 inches from beg, ending with a WS row.

Armhole shaping
At beg of next row, bind off 2 (4, 4, 4, 4) sts for armhole, then bind off 0 (2, 0, 2, 2) sts at armhole edge on next RS row. Work 1 row even.

Dec row (RS): K1, ssk, knit across.

Continue in St st dec as above at each armhole edge [every other row] 3 (4, 4, 6, 7) times. (37, 37, 44, 46, 51 sts)

Continue even in St st until piece measures approx 18½ (19, 19½, 20, 20½) inches from beg, ending with a RS Row.

Neck shaping
Row 1 (WS): Bind off 6 sts, purl across.

Row 2 (RS): Knit.

Row 3: Bind off 4 sts, purl across.

Row 4: Knit.

Row 5: Bind off 2 (3, 4, 4, 4) sts, purl across.

Row 6: Knit to last 3 sts, k2 tog, k1.

Row 7: Purl.

Rows 8–15: [Rep Rows 6 and 7] 4 times more. (20, 19, 25, 27, 32 sts)

Work even until piece measures same as back to shoulder ending with a WS row.

Bind off all sts.

Right Front
Work same as left front to Armhole shaping, ending with a RS row.

Armhole shaping
Bind off 2 (4, 4, 4, 4) sts for armhole, then bind off 0 (2, 0, 2, 2) sts at armhole edge next WS row.

Dec row (RS): Knit to last 3 sts, k2tog, k1.

Working in St st dec as above at each

armhole edge [every other row] 3 (4, 4, 6, 7) times. (37, 37, 44, 46, 51 sts)

Continue even in St st until piece measures approximately 18½ (19, 19½, 20, 20½) inches from beg, ending with a WS Row.

Neck shaping

Row 1 (RS): Bind off 6 sts, knit across.

Row 2: Purl.

Row 3: Bind off 4 sts, knit across.

Row 4: Purl.

Row 5: Bind off 2 (3, 4, 4, 4) sts, knit across.

Row 6: Purl.

Row 7: K1, ssk, knit across.

Row 8: Purl.

Rows 9–16: [Rep Rows 7 and 8] 4 times more. (20, 19, 25, 27, 32 sts)

Work even in St st until piece measures same as back to shoulder, ending with a RS row.

Bind off all sts.

Sleeves

Make 2

With smaller needles and B cast on 48 (48, 50, 50, 52) sts. Fasten off B.

With A, work in K1, p1 rib for approx 2 inches, ending with a WS row.

Change to larger needles.

Working in St st, inc 1 st by M1 each side [every 4th row] 0 (6, 13, 22, 24) times, then [every 6th row] 16 (13, 7, 1, 0) times. (80, 86, 90, 96, 100 sts)

Work even until piece measures approx 19½ (19¾, 19½, 19, 18) inches, ending with a WS row.

Bind off 2 (4, 4, 4, 4) sts at beg of next 2 rows, 0 (2, 0, 2, 2) sts at beg of next 2 rows, then dec each side [every other row] 4 (5, 5, 7, 8) times. (68, 64, 72, 70, 72 sts)

Bind off all sts.

Assembly

Sew shoulder seams.

Neck band

With RS facing, smaller needles and B, pick up and knit 92 (94, 96, 96, 96) sts evenly spaced around neckline, including sts from holder. Work in k1, p1 rib for approx ¾ inch. Bind off loosely in ribbing.

Button band

With RS facing, smaller needles and B, pick up and knit 90 (92, 94, 96, 98) sts evenly spaced along left front edge. Work in k1, p1 rib until band measures approximately ¾ inch. Bind off loosely in rib.

Place markers for 10 buttons evenly spaced along band with first and last marker ½ inch from top and bottom edge.

Buttonhole Band

With RS facing, smaller needles and B, pick up and knit 90 (92, 94, 96, 98) sts evenly along right front edge. Work in k1, p1 rib until band measures approximately ¼ inch.

Next row (buttonhole row): *Work in pat to marker, k2tog, yo; rep from * 9 times more, work in pat across.

Next row: Work in pat across working into back of each yo.

Continue in rib pat until band measures approx ¾ inches.

Bind off loosely in rib.

Finishing

Set in sleeves. Sew sleeve and side seams.

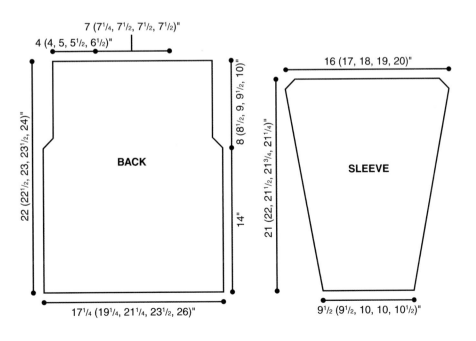

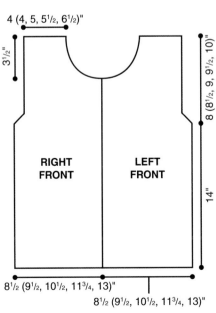

SHOPPING SPREE TANK

Design by Scarlet Taylor

Skill Level

EASY

Sizes

Woman's small (medium, large, extra-large, 2X-large) Instructions are given for smallest size, with larger sizes in parentheses. When only 1 number is given, it applies to all sizes.

Finished Measurements

Bust: 32 (36, 40, 45, 49½) inches
Length: 20½ (21, 21½, 22, 22½) inches

Materials

Worsted weight yarn (3.5 oz/186 yds/100g per skein): 2 (2, 3, 3, 3) skeins salsa #3270 (A) and 2 (2, 3, 3, 3) skeins gold #3215 (B)

Note: *Our photographed tank was made with TLC Cotton Plus.*

Size 7 (4.5mm) knitting needles

Size 8 (5mm) knitting needles or size needed to obtain gauge

Gauge

20 sts and 25 rows = 4 inches/10cm in St st with larger needles
To save time, take time to check gauge.

Special Abbreviations

Slip, slip, knit (ssk): Sl next 2 sts knitwise one at a time from left to right needle, insert LH needle through fronts of these sts and k2tog to dec 1 st.
Purl 2 together through back loops (p2tog-tbl): Purl next 2 sts tog through the back lps.

Pattern Stitch

Stripe

Row 1 (RS): With B, knit.
Row 2: Purl.
Row 3: With A, knit.
Row 4: Purl
Rep Rows 1–4 for pat.

Pattern Notes

Armhole and neck band edges are worked at the same time as the body. Carry yarns loosely along edge.
When changing colors, bring new color under and around working color to twist yarns on WS and prevent holes in work.

Back/Front

Make 2

With smaller needles and B cast on 80 (90, 100, 112, 124) sts. Fasten off B.

With A, work in k1, p1 rib for approx 3 inches, ending with a WS row.

Change to larger needles.

Work Stripe pat until piece measures approx 13½ inches from beg, ending with a Row 4.

Armhole shaping

Next row (RS): With B, p1, k1, p1; ssk, knit to last 5 sts, k2tog, join 2nd skein of B, p1, k1, p1.

Next row: K1, p1, k1, p2tog; purl to last 5 sts, p2tog-tbl, k1, p1, k1.

Continue in Stripe pat, working first and last 3 sts in rib pat as established with B and dec 1 st each side [every row] 9 (11, 8, 13, 4) times more, then [every other] row 0 (1, 4, 3, 11) times. (58, 62, 72, 76, 90 sts)

Continue even in pat, if necessary, until piece measures approx 15½ (16, 16½, 17, 18) inches from beg, ending with a Row 4.

Neck & shoulder shaping

Row 1 (RS): Continue in pat as established k16 (16, 21, 22, 27) sts, p1, k1, p1 (first shoulder); work k1, p1 rib across center 20 (24, 24, 26, 30) sts dec 1 st evenly across (neck band); p1, k1, p1, k13 (13, 18, 19, 24) sts, p1, k1, p1 (2nd shoulder).

Row 2: Continue in pats as established.

Row 3: Work edging in B, join A and k13 (13, 18, 19, 24) sts, join 2nd skein of B and work edging pat over 3 sts; with B bind off center 19 (23, 23, 25, 29) sts in rib for neck band; work 2nd strap edging over first 3 sts, join A and k13 (13, 18, 19, 24) sts, join B and work edging.

Working both straps at once with separate skeins of yarn, continue in pat as established, joining additional skeins as necessary, and working first and last 3 sts in rib in B for edgings, until piece measures approx 20½ (21, 21½, 22, 22½) inches ending with a WS row. Bind off

Finishing

Sew shoulder strap seams. Sew side seams. Weave in all ends.

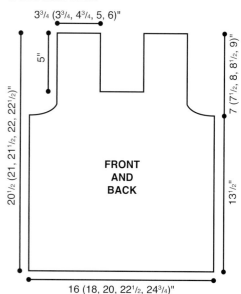

3¾ (3¾, 4¾, 5, 6)"

5"

7 (7½, 8, 8½, 9)"

20½ (21, 21½, 22, 22½)"

13½"

FRONT AND BACK

16 (18, 20, 22½, 24¾)"

IMPRESS THE BOARD

Design by Darla Sims

Skill Level

INTERMEDIATE

Sizes

Woman's small (medium, large, extra-large) Instructions are given for the smallest size, with larger sizes in parentheses. When only 1 number is given, it applies to all sizes.

Finished Measurement

Chest: 40 (44, 48, 52) inches

Materials

Worsted weight yarn (1.76 oz/98 yds/50g per ball): 12 (14, 14, 16) balls pink #3701

Note: Our photographed sweater was made with Mode Dea Dream.

Size 9 (5.5mm) knitting needles

Size 10 (6mm) knitting needles or size needed to obtain gauge

Size G/6/4mm crochet hook

7 (½-inch) pearl buttons

Stitch holders

Stitch markers

Gauge

15 sts and 22 rows = 4 inches/10cm in St st

To save time, take time to check gauge.

Pattern Stitch

Eyelet Cable (multiple of 7 sts + 1)

Note: Count sts on Rows 2 and 5 only.

Row 1 (RS): P1, *k1-tbl, p1, k2, p1, k1-tbl, p1; rep from * across.

Row 2: K1, *p1-tbl, k1, p2, k1, p1-tbl, k1; rep from * across.

Row 3: P1, *k1-tbl, p1, k1, yo, k1, p1, k1-tbl, p1; rep from * across.

Row 4: K1, *p1-tbl, k1, p3, k1, p1-tbl, k1; rep from * across.

Row 5: P1, *k1-tbl, p1, k3, pass 3rd st on right needle over first 2 sts, p1, k1-tbl, p1; rep from * across.

Rep Rows 2–5 for pat.

Back

With smaller needles, cast on 71 (78, 85, 92) sts.

Rows 1–21: Work Eyelet Cable pat.

Row 22: Purl.

Row 23 (inc row): Knit across, inc 9 (10, 11, 12) sts evenly spaced across row. (80, 88, 96, 104 sts)

Change to larger needles.

Work in St st until piece measure approx 14 (14½, 15, 15½) inches from beg, ending by working a WS row.

Armhole shaping

Bind off 10 (12, 13, 15) sts at beg of next 2 rows. (60, 64, 70, 74 sts)

Dec 1 st each end [every other row] 3 times. (54, 58, 64, 68 sts)

Work even until armhole measures 9 (9½, 10, 10½) inches, ending with a WS row.

Shoulder shaping

Bind off 5 (5, 6, 6) sts at beg of next 4 rows, bind off 6 sts at beg of next 2 rows. (22, 26, 28, 32 sts)

Bind off rem sts for neck.

Right Front

With smaller needles, cast on 36 (43, 43, 50) sts.

Rows 1–21: Work Eyelet Cable pat, ending with a Row 5 of pat.

Row 22: Purl to last 8 sts, place marker, work Row 2 of Eyelet Cable pat across last 8 sts.

Row 23 (inc row): Work Row 3 of Eyelet Cable pat across first 8 sts for band, knit rem sts, inc 10 (7, 11, 8) sts evenly spaced across. (46, 50, 54, 58 sts)

Change to larger needles.

Continue in pat as established working Eyelet Cable pat for center band and rem sts in St st until same length as back to armhole, ending by working a RS row.

Armhole shaping

Bind off 10 (12, 13, 15) sts at beg of next row. (36, 38, 41, 43 sts)

Dec 1 st at armhole edge on RS rows 3 times. (33, 35, 38, 40 sts)

Work even in pat as established until armhole measures 7 (7½, 8, 8½) inches, ending by working a WS row.

Neck shaping

Bind off 13 (15, 15, 17) sts at beg of next row for neck. (20, 20, 23, 23 sts)

Next row (WS): Work in pat across.

Next row (RS): Dec 1 st at neck edge, work in pat across.

Rep last 2 rows 3 (3, 4, 4) times. (16, 16, 18, 18 sts)

Work even, if necessary, until armhole measures 9 (9½, 10, 10½) inches, ending by working a RS row.

Shoulder shaping

Row 1 (WS): Bind off 5 (5, 6, 6) sts, work in pat across.

Row 2: Work in pat across.

Rows 3 and 4: Rep Rows 1 and 2.

Bind off rem 6 sts.

Left Front

With smaller needles, cast on 36 sts (43, 43, 50).

Rows 1–21: Work Eyelet Cable pat, ending with a Row 5 of pat.

Row 22: Work Row 2 of Eyelet Cable pat across first 8 sts, place marker, purl across.

Row 23 (inc row): Knit to marker, inc 10 (7, 11, 8) sts evenly spaced, work Row 3 of Eyelet Cable pat across last 8 sts. (46, 50, 54, 58)

Change to larger needles.

Continue in pat as established, working Eyelet Cable pat for center band and rem sts in St st until same length as back to armhole, ending by working a WS row.

Armhole shaping

Bind off 10 (12, 13, 15) sts at beg of next row. (36, 38, 41, 43 sts)

Dec 1 st at armhole edge each RS row 3 times. (33, 35, 38, 40 sts).

Work even in pat as established until armhole measures 7 (7½, 8, 8½) inches, ending by working a RS row.

Neck shaping

Bind off 13 (15, 15, 17) sts at beg of next row for neck. (20, 20, 23, 23 sts)

Next row (RS): Work in pat to last 2 sts, k2tog.

Next row: Work in pat across.

Rep last 2 rows 3 (3, 4, 4) times. (16, 16, 18, 18 sts)

Work even, if necessary, until armhole measures 9 (9½, 10, 10½) inches, ending by working a WS row.

Shoulder shaping

Row 1 (RS): Bind off 5 (5, 6, 6) sts work in pat across.

Row 2: Work in pat across.

Rows 3 and 4: Rep Rows 1 and 2.

Bind off rem 6 sts.

Sleeve

With smaller needles cast on 36 (36, 42, 42) sts.

Rows 1 (RS)–21: Work in Eyelet Cable pat, ending by working a Row 5.

Row 22: Purl.

Row 23: Knit inc 4 (6, 2, 4) sts evenly spaced across. (40, 42, 44, 46 sts)

Change to larger needles.

Work even in St st, inc 1 st each end [every 6th row] 10 times. (60, 62, 64, 66 sts)

American School of Needlework, Berne, IN 46711 • ASNpub.com

Work even until sleeve measures
17 inches, ending by working a RS row.

Cap Shaping
Bind off 10 (12, 13, 15) sts at beg next
2 rows. (40, 38, 38, 36 sts)

Dec 1 st each end [every RS row] 3 times.
(34, 32, 32, 30 sts)

Work 10 (12, 14, 16) rows even.

Dec 1 st, each end [every RS row] 10
times. (14, 12, 12, 10 sts)

Bind off rem sts.

Assembly
Sew shoulder seam. Set in sleeve. Sew
sleeve and side in 1 continuous seam.

Neck Edging
*Note: If not familiar with single crochet
(sc), see page 63.*

Hold with RS facing, join with sc at right
center front, work 19 (20, 21, 22) evenly
spaced to right shoulder, 19 (20, 21, 22) sc
across back neck, 19 (20, 21, 22) sc evenly
spaced along left neck edge to center front.

Finishing
Sew on buttons evenly spaced along front
edge. Use yarn overs of Eyelet Cable pat
as buttonholes.

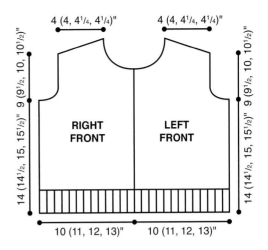

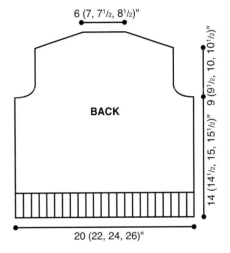

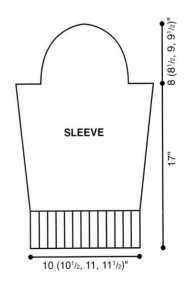

ADDED SPICE SCARF

Design by Cindy Adams

Skill Level

EASY

Finished Size

Approx 5 x 68 inches

Materials

Worsted weight yarn (6 oz/
278 yds/170g per skein):
1 skein persimmon
#3254 (A)

Worsted weight novelty yarn (1.76 oz/
89 yds/50g per ball): 1 ball sandy
#9117 (B)

Worsted weight cotton yarn (3.5
oz/178 yds/100g per skein): 1
ball red #3907 (C)

Worsted weight brushed yarn (3.5
oz/310 yds/100g per skein): 1
skein persimmon #4906 (D)

Note: *Our photographed scarf was
made with TLC Amore, Red Heart
Foxy, TLC cotton plus and Red
Heart Symphony.*

Size 10 (5.75mm) knitting needles
or size needed to obtain gauge

Gauge

12 sts = 4 inches (10cm)
Gauge is not critical to this project.

Special Abbreviation

Increase (inc): Inc 1 by knitting in
front and back of next st.

Pattern Notes

Change colors on a RS row.
Work increases and decreases on WS rows.

Scarf

With A, cast on 20 sts.

Row 1 (RS): Sl p1 wyif, knit across.

Row 2: Sl 1p wyif, inc, k15, k2tog, k1.

Rows 3–10: Rep Rows 1 and 2. Fasten off.

Rows 11–20: With B, rep Rows 1–10.

Rows 21–30: With C, rep Rows 1–10.

Rows 31 – 40: With D, rep rows 1 – 10.

[Rep Rows 1–40] 5 times more.

With A, rep Rows 1–10.

Bind off and weave in ends.

American School of Needlework, Berne, IN 46711 • ASNpub.com

GREEN-WITH-ENVY SCARF

Design by Cindy Adams

Skill Level

■□□□

BEGINNER

Finished Size

Approx 5 x 60 inches excluding fringe

Materials

Worsted weight yarn (6 oz/ 278 yds/170g per skein): 1 skein each dark thyme #3628 (A) and celery #3625 (B)

Bulky weight novelty yarn (1.76/89 yds/50g per skein): 1 skein grass #9630 (C)

Bulky weight novelty yarn (1.75 oz/ 71 yds/50g per skein): 1 skein mallard #81236 (D)

Note*: Our photographed scarf was made with TLC Amore, Red Heart Foxy and Bernat Boa.*

Size 10½ (6.5mm) 24-inch long circular needle

Gauge

10 sts = 4 inches (10cm) with worsted yarn

To save time, take time to check gauge.

Special Abbreviation

Knit Wrapping Twice (KW2): Knit next st wrapping yarn twice around needle. On next row drop extra wrap.

Pattern Notes

Leave an 8-inch tail to be included in fringe when attaching yarns.

Circular needle is used to accommodate stitches; do not join. Work back and forth in rows.

Scarf

With A, cast on 110 sts.

Rows 1–4: Knit.

Rows 5 and 6: With D, knit.

Row 7: With B, K1, *KW2; rep from * to last st, k1.

Row 8: Knit each st dropping 2nd wrap of each st.

Rows 9 and 10: With A, knit.

Rows 11–14: With C, knit.

Rows 15 and 16: With A, knit.

Rows 17–19: With D, knit.

Slide work to other end of needle.

Rows 20–24: With B, knit.

Slide work to other end of needle.

Row 25: With C, K1, *KW2; rep from * to last st, k1.

Row 26: Knit each st dropping 2nd wrap of each st.

Rows 27 and 28: With A, knit.

Fringe

Following Fringe instructions on page 60, make single knot fringe. Cut 15-inch strands of all yarns. Use 2 strands of assorted yarns and yarn ends for each knot. Tie evenly spaced across each short end.

FLOWER PINS

Designs by Barbara Venishnick

Skill Level

EASY

Finished Size

Approx 3½-inch diameter flower;
5 inches overall with leaves

Materials

Novelty eyelash yarn (1.5 oz/
57 yds/40g per ball):
1 ball confetti #206 (A) *or*
ribbon yarn (1.75 oz/110
yds/50g per ball): 1 ball #208
copper penny (A)

Worsted weight yarn (2.5 oz/168
yds/70g per ball): 1 ball lime
#194 (B) *or* (3 oz/197 yds/85g
per ball): 1 ball seaspray #123 (B)

*Note: Our photographed pins were
both made following the same
pattern. The furry flower is made
with Fun Fur and Micro Spun;
the ribbon flower is made with
Incredible and Wool-Ease, all by
Lion Brand Yarn.*

Size 5 (3.75mm) straight or 2
double-pointed needles (for fur
flower and leaves)

Size 8 (5mm) straight or 2 double-
pointed needles (for ribbon
flower and leaves)

1¼-inch-long pin back

Gauge

Gauge not critical to project.

Special Abbreviation

Make 1 (M1): Inc 1 by inserting LH
needle from back to front under the
horizontal strand between st just worked
and next st, knit into the front of lp.

Knit cast-on: Insert right needle
knitwise into the next st on LH needle,
knit but do not remove st from RH
needle, insert LH needle from right to
left into st and slide to LH needle.

Slip, slip, knit (ssk): Sl next 2 sts
knitwise one at a time front left to right
needle, insert LH needle through fronts
of these sts and k2 tog to dec 1 st.

Pattern Notes

The flower is made of a long strand of
fringe that is rolled up and tacked in
place. The leaves are made separately
and sewn to the back of the flower.

Flower

With A, cast on 9 sts, leaving a 24-inch
tail. P9, turn.

Bind off 7 sts, k2, turn.

*Note: Last st left on RH needle after
binding off counts as first st of k2.*

Row 1: P2.

Row 2: Knit cast on 7 sts, bind off 7 sts, k2.

[Rep Rows 1 and 2] 19 times. End last
row by binding off all 9 sts.

To form flower, hold string of fringe by
p2 base with RS facing. Roll stitched end
of fringe, keeping edge even (think of

rewinding a tape measure). As you wrap, sew petals in place at base, using long tail from cast on.

When all petals are secured, run threaded needle through entire roll in several places to keep back of flower flat.

Leaves
Make 2
Note: Slip all sts purlwise with yarn in front.

With B, cast on 3 sts.

Row 1 (RS): K3.

Row 2: K1, sl 1, k1.

Row 3: K1, [M1, k1] twice. (5 sts)

Row 4: K2, sl 1, k2.

Row 5: K1, M1, k3, M1, k1. (7 sts)

Row 6: K3, sl 1, k3.

Row 7: K1, M1, k5, M1, k1. (9 sts)

Row 8: K4, sl 1, k4.

Row 9: K1, M1, k7, M1, k1. (11 sts)

Row 10: K5, sl 1, k5.

Row 11: K11.

Rows 12 and 13: Rep Rows 10 and 11

Row 14: Rep Row 10.

Row 15: K1, ssk, k5, k2tog, k1. (9 sts)

Row 16: K4, sl 1, k4.

Row 17: K1, ssk, k3, k2tog, k1. (7 sts)

Row 18: K3, sl 1, k3.

Row 19: K1, ssk, k1, k2tog, k1. (5 sts)

Row 20: K2, sl 1, k2.

Row 21: Ssk, k1, k2tog. (3 sts)

Row 22: K1, sl 1, k1.

Row 23: Sl next 2 sts as if to k2tog, k1, p2sso.

Cut yarn and pull through last st. Fasten off.

Assembly
Sew leaves to back of flower. Sew pin back to center of underside.

CARMEN SHOULDER BAG

Design by Kara Guild for Bernat

Skill Level

BEGINNER

Finished Size

Approx 8 x 9 inches

Materials

Bulky weight yarn (1.75 oz/
    64 yds/50g per ball):
    2 balls wine #07430

Note: *Our photographed bag
    was made with Patons Carmen.*

Size 10½ (6.5mm) needles or size
    needed to obtain gauge

1 yd satin drapery cord

¼ yd lining fabric

Snap fastener (optional)

2 (3-inch) tassels (optional)

Sewing needle and matching thread

Gauge

12 sts and 28 rows = 4 inches/10cm in
garter st

To save time, take time to check gauge.

Bag

Cast on 26 sts and work garter st,
marking first row for WS, until work
measures 18 inches from beg, ending with
a WS row.

Bind off knitwise.

Assembly

Lining

Before sewing side seams of bag, mark
shape of bag on WS of lining fabric,
adding ⅝-inch seam allowance on all
sides. Cut out lining and sew sides.

Fold bag in half with WS of work tog.
Sew side seams, leaving a ¼-inch opening
at bottom for cord. Tuck ends of cord
into openings. With sewing thread and
needle, sew opening closed, securing end
of cord. Sew cord to side seams of bag.

Fold and sew lining along top edge of bag
½ inch from edge. Press lining to WS
along stitching line. If desired, sew snap
fastener to lining at center of top opening.

ZINGY ZEBRA PURSE

Design by Svetlana Avrakh

Skill Level

INTERMEDIATE

Finished Size

Approx 9 x 11 inches

Materials

Worsted weight yarn (3.5 oz/
  223 yds/100g per skein):
  1 skein each black #227
  (MC) and Aran #202
  (CC)

4 MEDIUM

*Note: Our photographed purse was
  made with Patons Classic Wool.*

Size 6 (4mm) needles
Size 7 (4.5mm) needles or size
  needed to obtain gauge
1 pair 6-inch wide purse handles
11x 22-inch piece of fabric for
  lining

Gauge

20 sts and 26 rows = 4 inches/10cm
in St st
To save time, take time to check gauge.

Pattern Notes

Pattern is worked from a chart, read knit (RS) rows from right to left and purl (WS) rows from left to right, noting increases for side shaping. To change color, bring new color under previous color to create a half-twist and prevent holes in work.

Front/Back

Make 2

With larger needles and MC, cast on 33 sts. Beg with a RS row and St st, work 2 rows.

Continuing in St st, work Rows 1–51 from chart. (57 sts)

Change to smaller needles.

Top Border

Next row: With MC, knit, dec 6 sts evenly spaced across row. (51 sts)

Knit 6 rows.

Bind off knitwise on WS.

Finishing

Cut 2 pieces of lining ½ inch larger than work on all sides. Sew side and bottom seams and hem top edge.

Sew sides and bottom of purse. Sew lining inside purse.

Place purse on flat surface and mark upper edge 1½ inches from each side. Sew handle to inside of purse at markers.

STITCH KEY
☐ MC (Black)
☐ CC (Aran)

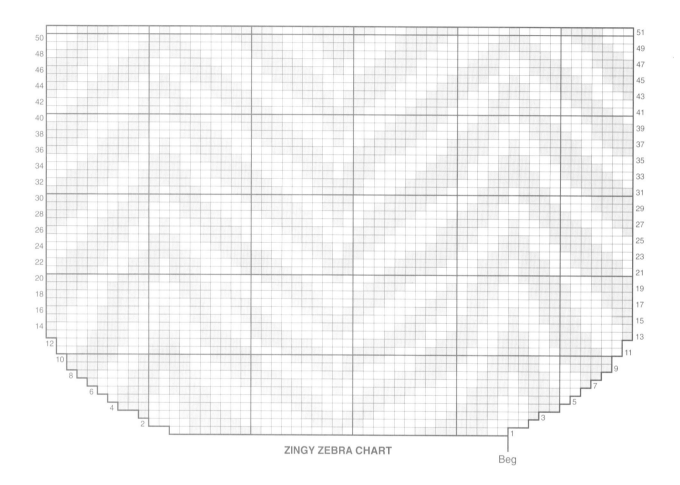

ZINGY ZEBRA CHART

Beg

BRING ON THE BLING

Design by Darla Sims

Skill Level

INTERMEDIATE

Sizes

Woman's small (medium, large, extra-large) Instructions are given for smallest size, with larger sizes in parentheses. When only 1 number is given, it applies to all sizes.

Finished Measurements

Chest: 38 (42, 46, 50) inches

Materials

Super Bulky weight fur yarn (1.75 oz/77 yds/50g per ball): 6 (7, 7, 8) balls hip #35142 (MC)

Worsted weight yarn (3.5 oz/ 166 yds/100g per ball): 1 (1, 2, 2) balls skipper #04134 (CC)

Note: Our photographed sweater was made with Bernat Eyelash and Bernat Satin.

Size 13 (9mm) circular knitting needle or size needed to obtain gauge

Size H/8/5mm crochet hook

Stitch holder

5 crystal buttons

Sewing needle and matching thread

Gauge

12 sts = 4 inches/10cm in garter st
To save time, take time to check gauge.

Pattern Notes

Body is made in one piece to underarm. Circular needle is used to accommodate sts, do not join. Work back and forth in rows.

Body

With MC, cast on 106 (118, 132, 144) sts.

Work in garter st (knit every row) until piece measures 12 inches.

Left/Right Front

Work across 26 sts (30, 33, 36) sts; place center 54 (58, 66, 72) sts on st holder;

join 2nd ball and work across rem 26 (30, 33, 36) sts.

Working both fronts at the same time, cast on 3 sts at beg of armhole edge for sleeves [every other row] twice. (32, 36, 39, 42 sts for each front)

Work even in garter st until armhole measures 4½ (5, 5½, 6) inches.

Neck shaping

At neck edge, bind off 8 (8, 9, 9) sts, complete row. (24, 28, 30, 33 sts on each front)

Dec 1 st at neck edge only, [every other row] 3 times. (21, 25, 27, 30 sts on each front)

Work even until armhole measures 7½ (8, 8½, 9) inches.

Bind off all sts.

Back

Sl sts from st holder to needle.

Continue in garter st, casting on 3 sts at the beg of next 4 rows. (66, 70, 78, 84 sts)

Work even in garter st until back is same length as front.

Bind off all sts.

Assembly

Sew shoulder seams. Sew sleeve and side in one continuous seam.

Note: *If not familiar with a single crochet (sc), refer to page 63.*

Armhole edging

Rnd 1: With RS facing and beg at underarm seam, with CC work 36 (38, 40, 42) sc evenly around sleeve edge, join in first sc.

Rnds 2–4: Ch 1, sc in same st as joining and in each sc around, join in first sc. At end of Rnd 4, fasten off.

Lower edging

Rnd 1: With RS facing and lower edge at top, beg at center front, with CC, work 94 (98, 102, 104) sc evenly spaced along lower edge. Turn.

Rnds 2–4: Ch 1, sc in each sc across. At end of Rnd 4, fasten off.

Front edging

Rnd 1: Hold with RS of right front facing, beg at lower front, with CC, work 54 (58, 66, 72) sc to neck shaping, work 3 sc in corner st, 32 (32, 24, 24) sc around neck, 3 sc in corner st, 54 (58, 66, 72) along left front to bottom of front. Turn.

Rnds 2–4: Ch 1, sc in each sc. Turn.

Place 5 markers evenly spaced along right front for button loops.

Rnd 5: Ch 1, *sc to marker, ch 2, sl st in 3rd st to right of hook, 3 sc in loop (button loop); rep from * 4 times more, sc across. Fasten off.

Sew buttons opposite button loops.

CHARITABLE-EVENT PONCHETTE

Design by Scarlet Taylor

Skill Level

EASY

Finished Measurements

Circumference at lower edge: 48 (51¾, 55½, 59¼) inches

Circumference at shoulder: 35¼ (39, 42½, 46½) inches

Length: 14¼ (14¾, 15¼, 15¾) inches

Materials

Bulky weight yarn (1.76 oz/70 yds per ball) 7 (8, 9, 10) balls sandpiper #0009

Note: Our photographed cape was made with Caron Feathers.

Size 7 (4.5mm) circular knitting needle (for cowl neck)

Size 8 (5mm) circular knitting needle or size needed to obtain gauge

Stitch markers

Gauge

15 sts and 23 rows = 4 inches/10cm in St st using larger needles

To save time, take time to check gauge.

Pattern Notes

Circular needle used to accommodate number of sts. The body is worked back and forth in rows; do not join.

Cowl collar is worked in rnds.

Ponchette

With smaller needle, cast on 180 (194, 208, 222) sts.

Knit 3 rows.

Change to larger needle.

Beg with WS row, work 8 rows in St st.

Dec row (RS): K12 (12, 12, 16), place marker, k2tog, *k20 (22, 24, 25), place marker, k2tog; rep from *6 times more, k12 (12, 12, 15). (172, 186, 200, 214 sts)

Work 7 rows in St st.

Dec row (RS): *Knit to next marker, sl marker, k2tog, rep from * to last marker, sl marker, k2tog, knit to across. (164, 178, 192, 206 sts)

Rep last 8 rows 4 times more. (132, 146, 160, 174 sts)

Work even until piece measures approx 10 (10½, 11, 11½) inches from beg, ending with a WS row.

Neck & shoulder shaping

Next row (RS): K11 (9, 10, 8), k2tog, [k4, k2tog] 18 (21, 23, 26) times, k11 (9, 10, 8). (113, 124, 136, 147 sts)

Work 7 rows even.

Next row (RS): K11 (9, 10, 8), k2tog, [k3, k2tog] 18 (21, 23, 26) times, k10 (8, 9, 7). (94, 102, 112, 120 sts)

Work 7 rows even.

Next row: K10 (8, 9, 7), k2tog, [k2, k2tog] 18 (21, 23, 26) times, k10 (8, 9, 7). (75, 80, 88, 93 sts)

Work 7 rows even.

Next row: K10 (8, 9, 7), k2tog, [k1, k2tog] 18 (21, 23, 26) times, k9 (7, 8, 6). (56, 58, 64, 66 sts)

Leave sts on needles.

Assembly

Sew back seam.

Cowl Collar

With RS facing, sl sts from needle onto smaller circular needle, place marker for beg of rnd, and join. Work in rnds of St st (knit every rnd) for 2 inches.

Next rnd: Knit inc 5 sts evenly spaced. (61, 63, 69, 71 sts)

Work even until collar measures 4 inches.

Next rnd: Knit inc 5 sts evenly spaced. (66, 68, 74, 76 sts)

Work even until collar measures 7 inches.

Next rnd: Knit inc 5 sts evenly spaced. (71, 73, 79, 81 sts)

Work even until collar measures 9 inches.

Bind off loosely with larger needle.

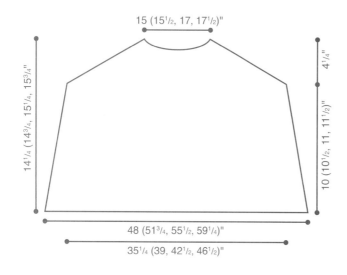

15 (15½, 17, 17½)"

14¼ (14¾, 15¼, 15¾)"

10 (10½, 11, 11½)"

4¼"

48 (51¾, 55½, 59¼)"

35¼ (39, 42½, 46½)"

RUFFLED ROMANCE

Design by Darla Sims

Skill Level

INTERMEDIATE

Sizes

Woman's small (medium, large, extra-large) Instructions are given for smallest size, with larger sizes in parentheses. When only 1 number is given, it applies to all sizes.

Finished Measurement

Chest: 40 (44, 48, 52) inches

Materials

Bulky weight yarn (3 oz/122 yds/85g per skein): 6 (7, 8, 9) skeins rose #210-140

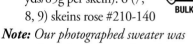

Note: Our photographed sweater was made with Lion Brand Suede.

Size 9 (5.5mm) straight and circular knitting needles

Sizes 10 (6mm) knitting needles or size needed to obtain gauge

Purchased brooch (optional)

Gauge

6 sts and 7 rows = 2 inches/5cm in St st with larger needles

To save time, take time to check gauge.

Special Abbreviations

Slip, slip, knit (ssk): Sl next 2 sts knitwise one at a time from left to right needle, insert LH needle through fronts of these sts and k2tog to dec 1 st.

Increase (inc): Inc 1 by knitting in front and back of next st.

Back

With larger needles, cast on 60 (66, 72, 78) sts.

Row 1 (RS): Knit.

Row 2: Purl.

Rep Rows 1 and 2 once more.

Next row (dec row): K1, k2tog, knit to last 3 sts, ssk, k1. (58, 64, 70, 76 sts)

Continue in St st, dec 1 st each end [every 6th row] as above 3 times. (52, 58, 64, 70 sts)

Work 4 rows even in St st.

Continue in St st, inc 1 st each end, [every 4th row] 4 times. (60, 66, 72, 78 sts)

Work even until piece measures 22 (22½, 23, 23½) inches.

Bind off all sts.

Right Front

With larger needles, cast on 30 (33, 36, 39) sts.

Row 1 (RS): Knit.

Row 2: Purl.

Rep Rows 1 and 2 once more.

Next row (dec row): Knit to last 3 sts, ssk, k1.

Continue in St st, dec 1 st side edge only [every 6th row] 3 times. (26, 29, 32, 35 sts)

Work 4 rows even in St st.

Continue in St st, inc 1 st side edge only [every 4th row] 4 times. (30, 33, 36, 39 sts)

Work even until piece measures approx 13 inches, ending by working a WS row.

Neck shaping

Continue in St st, dec 1 st by k2tog at neck edge only, 9 (9, 10, 10) times. (21, 24, 26, 29 sts)

Work even until same length as back.

Bind off all sts.

Left Front

With larger needles, cast on 30 (33, 36, 39) sts.

Row 1 (RS): Knit.

Row 2: Purl.

Rep Rows 1 and 2 once more.

Next row (dec row): K1, k2tog, knit across.

Continue in St st, dec 1 st side edge only [every 6th row] 3 times. (26, 29, 32, 35 sts)

Work 4 rows even in St st.

Continue in St st, inc 1 st every side edge [every 4th row] 4 times. (30, 33, 36, 39 sts)

Work even until piece measures approx 13 inches, ending by working a RS row.

Neck shaping

Continuing to work in St st, dec 1 st by ssk at neck edge only, 9 (9, 10, 10) times. (21, 24, 26, 29 sts)

Work even until same length as back.

Bind off all sts.

Assembly

Sew shoulder seams.

Sleeves

Place markers 9 (9½, 10, 10½) inches from shoulder seam on each side of front and back. With larger needles, pick up and knit 54 (58, 60, 64) sts between markers.

Work 2 inches even in St st.

Dec 1 st each end [every 4th row] 12 (13, 13, 14) times. (30, 32, 34, 36 sts)

Work even in St st until sleeve measures 13½ inches.

Bind off all sts.

Sleeve ruffle

With smaller needles, pick up and knit 30 sts (32, 34, 36) across lower sleeve edge.

Row 1 (WS): Purl.

Row 2 (RS): Inc in each st. (60, 64, 68, 72 sts)

Row 3: Purl.

Row 4: Knit, wrapping yarn twice around needle for each st.

Row 5: Purl, dropping extra wrap.

Bind off knitwise.

Finishing

Sew sleeve and side in one continuous seam.

Lower edge ruffle

With circular needle, pick up and knit in each st across lower edge of cardigan.

Work Rows 1–5 of sleeve ruffle.

Front ruffle

Hold with RS of right front facing, with circular needle, pick up and knit 40 sts from bottom of right front to V-neck shaping, pick up and knit 18 (20, 22, 24) sts from V-neck shaping to shoulder seam, pick up and knit 19 (20, 21, 22) sts across back of neck, pick up and knit 18 (20, 22, 24) sts from shoulder seam to V-neck shaping, pick up and knit 40 sts to bottom of left front.

Work Rows 1–5 of Sleeve Ruffle.

Sew lower ruffle and front ruffle tog.

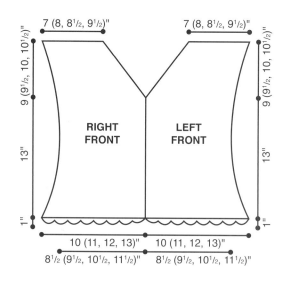

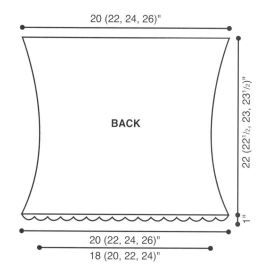

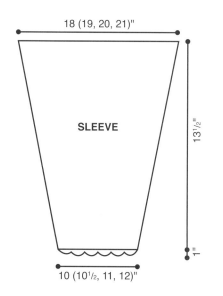

WORK-IT-OUT WARMERS

Design by Cindy Adams

Skill Level

INTERMEDIATE

Size

One size fits most

Finished Measurement

Approx 17 inches long

Materials

Bulky weight yarn (5 oz/255
    yds/140g per ball): 1 skein
    Westport shades #26949

*Note: Our photographed warmers were
    made with Bernat Soft Bouclé.*

Size 9 (5.5mm) double-pointed or
    small circular needles

Stitch marker

Gauge

12 sts = 4 inches/10cm in St st
To save time, take time to check gauge.

Special Abbreviation

Increase (inc): Inc 1 st by knitting in
front and back of next st.

Slip, slip, knit (ssk): Sl next 2 sts
knitwise one at a time from left to right
needle, insert LH needle through fronts
of these sts and k2tog to dec 1 st.

Leg Warmer

Make 2

Cast on 32 sts, join without twisting and
mark beg of rnd.

Rnds 1–12: Work in k2, p2 ribbing.

Rnd 13 (inc rnd): *K3, inc; rep from *
around. (40 sts)

Knit in rnds until piece measures
15 inches from beg or 3 inches less than
desired length.

Next rnd (dec rnd): *K3, ssk; rep from *
around. (32 sts)

Rep Rnds 1–12.

Bind off loosely in ribbing.

YOGA MAT
Design by Cindy Adams

Skill Level

EASY

Finished Size
24 x 58 inches

Materials
Super bulky weight yarn
(6 oz/108 yds/170g
per skein): 6 skeins
fisherman #099

Note: *Our photographed mat was
made with Lion Brand Wool-Ease
Thick & Quick.*

Size 11 (8mm) knitting needles
Stitch markers

Gauge
10 sts = 4 inches/10cm in pat

Pattern Stitch

Diamond

Row 1 (RS): K4, [p1, k7] 5 times, p1, k4.

Row 2: P3, [k1, p1, k1, p5] 5 times, k1, p1, k1, p3.

Row 3: K2, *p1, k3; rep from * to last 3 sts, p1, k2.

Row 4: P1, *k1, p5, k1, p1; rep from * across.

Row 5: P1, *k7, p1; rep from * across.

Row 6: Rep Row 4.

Row 7: Rep Row 3.

Row 8: Rep Row 2.

Rep Rows 1–8 for pat.

Yoga Mat
Cast on 59 sts.

Lower Border
Row 1 (WS): Sl 1p wyif, *p1, k1; rep from * across.

Rows 2–7: Rep Row 1.

Row 8 (RS): Sl 1p wyif, p1, k1, p1, k1, place marker, k49, place marker, k1, p1, k1, p1, k1.

Row 9: Sl 1p wyif, p1, k1, p1, k1, sl marker, p49, sl marker, k1, p1, k1, p1, k1.

Body
Continue to work seed st as established on first and last 5 sts and Diamond pat on center 49 sts.

Rep Rows 1–8 of Diamond pat until mat measures approx 56 inches from beg or 2 inches less than desired length.

Rep Row 1.

Upper Border
Rep Row 9 of lower border.

Rep Rows 1–7 of lower border.

Bind off all sts.

EVENING INTERLUDE

Design by Nazanin Fard

Skill Level

EASY

Finished Size

18 x 30 inches without fringe

Materials

Sport weight yarn (4 oz/113g per skein): 2 skeins ocean #0995

Note: *Our photographed table runner was made with Red Heart LusterSheen.*

Size 5 (3.75mm) knitting needles
Size E/4/3.5mm crochet hook

Gauge

24 sts and 20 ridge = 4 inches/10 cm in garter stitch
To save time, take time to check gauge.

Pattern Note

To have a nice edge on both sides for crocheting, sl the first st as if to purl.

Table Runner

Cast on 109 sts.

Knit 4 rows.

Row 1 (RS): Knit.

Row 2: Sl 1p, k4, p1, *K5, p1; rep from * to last st, p1.

Row 3–8: Rep Rows 1 and 2.

Row 9: Knit.

Row 10: Sl 1p, k2, * p1, k5; rep from * to last 4 sts, p1, k3.

Row 11–16: Rep Rows 9 and 10.

Rep Rows 1–16 until piece measures 30 inches.

Knit 4 rows.

Bind off loosely.

Finishing

Note: *If not familiar with single crochet stitch refer to page 61.*

Hold with RS facing and one long edge at top, with crochet hook, join in upper right-hand corner.

Row 1 (RS): Ch 1, sc in end of every row along edge.

Row 2: Ch 1, working from left to right across row, reverse sc across. Fasten off.

Rep along the other long edge.

Block runner to size.

Fringe

Following Fringe instructions on page 60, make single knot fringe. Cut 8-inch stands. Use 2 strands for each knot. Tie knot in every other st across each short end of runner. Trim ends even.

BYOB BAG

Design by Lorna Miser

Skill Level

EASY

Size

Approx 13 inches tall x 11 inches in circumference (16 inches tall x 13 inches in circumference) Instructions are given for smaller size, with larger size in parentheses. When only 1 number is given, it applies to both sizes.

Materials

Bulky weight yarn (4 oz/140 yds/113g per skein): 1 skein newport #3872

Note: Our photographed bottle cover was made with Red Heart Casual Cot'n.

Size 7 (4.5mm) knitting needles or size needed to obtain gauge

Assorted beads for ends of tie (optional)

Gauge

14 sts and 20 rows = 4 inches/10cm in St st

To save time, take time to check gauge.

Bottle Cover

Cast on 45 (56) sts.

Row 1 (RS): Purl.

Row 2: K6, yo, k2tog, knit across.

Rep Rows 1 and 2 until piece measures approx 11 (13) inches from cast-on edge.

Bind off all sts loosely.

Bottom

Row 1 (RS): Hold with RS facing, pick up and knit 36 (42) sts (2 sts for every 3 rows) along side opposite yo edge.

Row 2 and all even-numbered rows: Knit.

Row 3: [K1, k2tog] across. (24, 27 sts)

Row 5: [K1, k2tog] across. (16, 18 sts)

Row 7: [K2 (1), k2tog] across. (12 sts)

Row 9: [K2tog] across. (6 sts)

Cut yarn leaving an 18-inch end. Thread end through needle and weave through rem sts, gathering as you weave; secure end. Sew seam as flat as possible, butting edges tog. Sew side seam.

Tie

Make twisted cord (see page 60) about 20 inches long. Weave in and out of eyelets at top edge, beg and ending opposite seam.

Make overhand knot approx 2 inches from each end of cord. If desired, thread 3 assorted colored beads on each strand of cord. Tie knot below beads to hold in place.

POTLUCK PERFORMERS

Design by Lorna Miser

Skill Level

EASY

Finished Sizes

Oven mitt: One size fits most
Pot holder: 8 x 8 inches

Materials

Bulky weight yarn (4 oz/
140 yds/113g per skein):
2 skeins #3937 Grand
Canyon (1 skein for oven mitt
and 1 skein for pot holder)

Worsted weight cotton yarn:
small amount light rose
#3706 (for flower trim)

*Note: Our photographed set
was made with Red Heart Casual
Cot'n and TLC Cotton Plus.*

Size 7 (4.5 mm) knitting needles or
size needed to obtain gauge
Stitch marker
Tapestry needle

Gauge

12 sts and 22 rows = 4 inches/10cm in
seed st with double strand of yarn
To save time, take time to check gauge.

Special Abbreviations

Slip, slip, knit (ssk): Sl next 2 sts
knitwise one at a time from left to right
needle, insert LH needle through fronts
of these sts and k2tog to dec 1 st.
Increase (inc): Inc 1 st by knitting in
front and back of next st.

Pattern Stitch

Seed Stitch

(odd number of sts)

Row 1: K1 (p1, k1) across.
Rep Row 1 for pat.

Pattern Note

Yarn is used double throughout.

Oven Mitt

Hand

With 2 strands of yarn held tog, cast on
29 sts.

Work even in Seed st pat until piece
measures 8½ inches from beg.

Shape top

Row 1: K1, k2tog, [p1, k1] 4 times, p1,
ssk, k1, k2tog, [p1, k1] 4 times, p1, ssk, k1.

Row 2: K1, k1, [p1, k1] 5 times, p1, [k1,
p1] 5 times, k2.

Row 3: K1, k2tog, k1, [p1, k1] 3 times,
k1, ssk, k1, k2tog, k1, [p1, k1] 3 times,
k1, ssk, k1.

Row 4: K1, [p1, k1] 4 times, p3, k1, [p1,
k1] 4 times.

Row 5: K1, k2tog, [p1, k1] twice, p1, ssk,
k1, k2tog, [p1, k1] twice, p1, ssk, k1.

Bind off all sts.

Thumb

With 2 strands of yarn held tog, cast on
7 sts.

Work even in seed st for 3½ inches.

Thumb shaping

Row 1 (inc row): K1, inc, k1, p1, k1,
inc, k1.

Row 2: K2, [p1, k1] 3 times, k1.

Row 3: K1, inc, [p1, k1] twice, p1, inc, k1.

Row 4: K1, [p1, k1] 4 times, k1.

Row 5 (inc row): K1, inc, [k1, p1] 3
times, k1, inc, k1.

Row 6: K2, [p1, k1] 5 times, k1.

Mark end of last row for seam.

Work even in Seed st pat as established
for 4 rows.

Next row (dec row): [K2tog, p2tog] 6
times, k1.

Next row: K1, [p1, k1] 6 times.

Next row (dec row): K2tog, p2tog,
k2tog, k1.

Bind off.

Finishing

Fold hand in half and fold thumb in half.
Sew edges of hand and thumb tog up to
thumb marker. Above the marker, sew
the thumb edges tog then sew hand edges
tog. Referring to photo for placement,
with cotton yarn make daisy sts to form
flower (see Fig. 1).

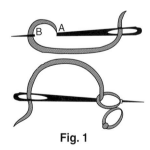

Fig. 1

To make Daisy: Bring needle up at A,
reinsert needle at A. Bring needle up at B at
desired length of loop and pull thread until
loop is formed. Stitch down over top of loop.

Pot Holder

With 2 strands of yarn held tog, cast on 21 sts. Work in Seed Stitch pat until piece measures 8 inches from beg.

Next Row: Cast on 7 sts. Bind off 6 sts, move st from right needle to left needle, knit 2tog and continue to bind off all rem sts.

Referring to photo for placement, with cotton yarn work daisy as for Oven Mitt in one corner.

POTLUCK HOSTESS

Design by Lorna Miser

Skill Level

EASY

Finished Size

One size fits most.

Materials

Bulky weight yarn (4 oz/ 140 yds/113g per skein): 4 skeins Grand Canyon #3937

Worsted weight cotton yarn: small amount light rose #3706 (for flower trim)

Note: *Our photographed set was made with Red Heart Casual Cot'n and TLC Cotton Plus.*

Size 7 (4.5mm) knitting needles or size needed to obtain gauge

Size 7 (4.5mm) 2 double-pointed needles (dpn) for I-cord ties

Tapestry needle

Gauge

14 sts and 20 rows = 4 inches/10cm in St st

To save time, take time to check gauge.

Apron

Cast on 77 sts.

Knit 4 rows.

Work in rev St st for 6 inches (pocket).

Change to St st and work for 14 inches, ending with a purl row.

Bind off 7 sts at beg of next 2 rows.

Next row (RS): K1, k2tog, knit to last 3 sts, ssk, k1.

Next row: Purl.

Rep last 2 rows until 35 sts rem.

Work even piece measures 9 inches from bound off sts.

Knit 4 rows.

Cast on 7 sts. Bind off 6 sts, move st from right needle to left needle, k2tog and continue to bind off all rem sts.

I-cord ties

Neck

With dpn, cast on 3 sts, *slide sts to other end of needle, pull yarn across WS of work, k3; rep from * until I-cord measures approx 20 inches long. Place sts on small safety pin and check length before binding off. Attach cast-on end to the neck edge of the apron, opposite loop. Place cord around back of neck, measure length and adjust as necessary. To wear, pull end through the loop and tie a loose knot.

Waist

Make 2

With dpn, cast on 3 sts, *slide sts to other end of needle, pull yarn across WS of work, k3; rep from * until I-cord measures approx 36 inches long, slide sts to other end of needle and bind off.

Attach 1 tie to each side of the apron where the shaping begins.

To wear, wrap each cord around the back, continue around to the front and tie ends tog in front.

Pocket

Fold pocket section up along change from Rev St st to St st and pin in place.

Side edgings

Row 1 (RS): Hold with RS facing and neck edge to right, beg at neck edge, pick up and knit 37 sts along shaped edge to waist, 45 sts from waist to folded hem.

Row 2: Knit.

Bind off all sts.

Rep along for opposite edge, picking up 45 from folder edge to waist and 37 sts from waist to neck edge.

Finishing

With matching yarn, sew vertically through both layers to divide into 3 pocket sections.

Referring to photo for placement, with cotton yarn make daisy sts to form flower (see Fig. 1).

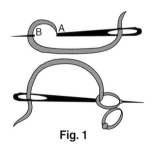

Fig. 1

To make Daisy: Bring needle up at A, reinsert needle at A. Bring needle up at B at desired length of loop and pull thread until loop is formed. Stitch down over top of loop.

LET'S GET TOGETHER

Design by Nazanin Fard

Skill Level

EASY

Finished Sizes

Casserole carrier: 7 wide x 11 inches long x 2½ inches high

Table mat: 13 inches square

Materials

Worsted weight cotton yarn (3.5 oz/178 yds/100g per ball): 3 balls spruce #3503 (A), 1 ball kiwi #3643 (B)

Note: Our photographed set was made with TLC Cotton Plus.

Size 8 (5mm) knitting needles

Size 10 (6mm) straight and circular knitting needles or size needed to obtain gauge

Size G/6/4mm crochet hook

Stitch markers

12 (0.5mm) pearl beads

Liquid fabric stiffener

Sewing needle and matching thread

Elastic thread

Gauge

14 sts = 4 inches/10cm in garter st with double strand on larger needles

24 sts and 32 rows = 4 inches/10cm in St st with single strand on smaller needle

To save time, take time to check gauge.

Special Abbreviations

Make 1 (M1): Inc 1 by inserting LH needle under horizontal strand between st just worked and next st, knit through back lp.

Increase (inc): Inc 1 by knitting in front and back of the next st.

Slip, slip, knit (ssk): Sl next 2 sts knitwise one at a time from left to right needle, insert LH needle through fronts of these sts and k2tog to dec 1 st.

Pattern Notes

Sl the first st on every row as if to purl. This will help with picking up sts for the edge.

Casserole carrier

With larger needles and double strand of A, cast on 24 sts.

Row 1: Knit.

Row 2: Sl 1p, M1, knit to last st, M1, k1. (26 sts)

Row 3: Knit.

Row 4: Rep Row 2. (28 sts)

Rows 5–60: Knit slipping the first st in each row purlwise.

Row 61: Sl 1p, ssk, knit to last 3 sts, k2tog, k1. (26 sts)

Row 62: Knit.

Row 63: Rep Row 61. (24 sts)

Row 64: Knit.

Place 24 sts on circular needle, pick up and knit 31 sts across one long edge, 24 sts across next short edge and 31 sts across other long edge, place marker. Join. (110 sts)

Note: When working in garter st in rnds, knit one rnd and purl one rnd.

Work in garter st for 2½ inches.

Bind off all sts loosely. Do not cut yarn.

Edging

Note: If not familiar with reverse single crochet (reverse sc), refer to page 63.

With crochet hook and RS facing you, work 1 rnd of reverse sc around the top edge.

Finishing

Dilute equal amount of fabric stiffener and water. Place the casserole carrier in the solution and let it sit for a couple of minutes. Squeeze out the excess fabric stiffener. Wrap the glass casserole dish in plastic bag and place it on a dry spot face down. Place the casserole carrier on top to take the shape of the dish. Let dry thoroughly.

Flower

Petal

With (B) and smaller needle, cast on 5 sts.

Row 1: Inc, k3, inc. (7 sts)

Row 2 and all even-numbered rows: Purl.

Row 3: Inc, k5, inc. (9 sts)

Row 5: Ssk, k5, k2tog. (7 sts)

Row 7: Ssk, k3, k2tog. (5 sts)

Row 8: P2tog, p1, p2tog. (3 sts)

Fasten off leaving sts on needle.

Rep making 5 more petals. (18 sts on needle)

Row 9: K2tog; rep from * across. (9 sts)

Row 10: *P2tog; rep from * across. (5 sts)

Fasten leaving approx 10-inch end. Thread end through needle and weave through all sts on needle. Pull tight and secure.

Leaf

Make 2

Cast on 5 sts.

Row 1: Knit.

Row 2: Purl.

Row 3: Inc, knit to last st needle inc. (11 sts at the end of row 7)

Rows 4–7: [Rep Rows 2 and 3] twice.

Row 8: Purl.

Row 9: Ssk, knit to last 2 sts, k2tog. (9 sts at the end of row 13)

Row 10: Purl.

Rows 11 and 12: Rep Rows 9 and 10.

Row 13: Rep Row 9.

Row 14: P2tog, p1, p2tog. (3 sts)

Row 15: K3tog. Fasten off.

With sewing needle and thread, sew 6 pearls in the center of flower. Referring to photo, sew edge of one flower to casserole carrier. Sew leaves on each side of flower.

Weave elastic thread through top edge of carrier and tighten as necessary to fit casserole dish.

Table Mat

With larger straight needles and double strand of A, cast on 35 sts.

Knit 60 rows for 30 ridges, working last row: k1, place marker, k33, place marker, k1.

Change to circular needle.

Rnd 1: Place marker, pick up and knit 30 sts across next side, place marker, pick up 1 st in corner, place marker, pick up 33 sts across next side, place marker, pick up 1 st in corner, place marker, pick up 30 sts across next side. Join. (130 sts)

Rnd 2 and all even-numbered rnds: Purl.

Rnd 3: Sl marker, yo, k1, yo, sl marker, k33, sl marker, yo, k1, yo, sl marker, k30, sl marker, yo, k1, yo, sl marker, k33, sl marker, yo, k1, yo, sl marker, k30. (138 sts)

Note: *Continue to sl markers as you come to them.*

Rnd 5: Yo, k3, yo, k33, yo, k3, yo, k30, yo, k3, yo, k33, yo, k3, yo, k30. (146 sts)

Rnd 7: Yo, k5, yo, k33, yo, k5, yo, k30, yo, k5, yo, k33, yo, k5, yo, k30. (154sts)

Rnd 9: Yo, k7, yo, k33, yo, k7, yo, k30, yo, k7, yo, k33, yo, k7, yo, k30. (162 sts)

Rnd 10: Purl.

Bind off all sts loosely. Do not cut yarn.

Note: *If not familiar with reverse single crochet (reverse sc), refer to page 63.*

With crochet hook work one rnd of reverse sc around the table mat.

Fasten off.

Finishing

Make Flower and Leaves as for Casserole Carrier.

KNITTING BASICS

Basic Stitches

Garter Stitch

On straight needles knit every row. When working in the round on circular or double-pointed needles, knit one round then purl one round.

Stockinette Stitch

On straight needles knit right-side rows and purl wrong-side rows. When working on circular or double-pointed needles, knit all rounds.

Reverse Stockinette Stitch

On straight needles purl right-side rows and knit wrong-side rows. On circular or double-pointed needles, purl all rounds.

Ribbing

Combining knit and purl stitches within a row to give stretch to the garment. Ribbing is most often used for the lower edge of the front and back, the cuffs and neck edge of garments.

The rib pattern is established on the first row. On subsequent rows the knit stitches are knitted and purl stitches are purled to form the ribs.

Reading Pattern Instructions

Before beginning a pattern, look through it to make sure you are familiar with the abbreviations that are used.

Some patterns may be written for more than one size. In this case the smallest size is given first and others are placed in parentheses. When only one number is given, it applies to all sizes.

You may wish to highlight the numbers for the size you are making before beginning. It is also helpful to place a self-adhesive sheet on the pattern to note any changes made while working the pattern.

Measuring

To measure pieces, lay them flat on a smooth surface. Take the measurement in the middle of the piece. For example, measure the length to the armhole in the center of the front or back piece, not along the outer edge where the edges tend to curve or roll.

Gauge

The single most important factor in determining the finished size of a knit item is the gauge. Although not as important for flat, one-piece items, it is important when making a clothing item that needs to fit properly.

It is important to make a stitch gauge swatch about 4 inches square with recommended patterns and needles before beginning.

Measure the swatch. If the number of stitches and rows are fewer than indicated under "Gauge" in the pattern, your needles are too large. Try another swatch with smaller-size needles. If the number of stitches and rows are more than indicated under "Gauge" in the pattern, your needles are too small. Try another swatch with larger-size needles.

Continue to adjust needles until correct gauge is achieved.

Working From Charts

When working with more than one color in a row, sometimes a chart is provided to follow the pattern. On the chart each square represents one stitch. A key is given indicating the color or stitch represented by each color or symbol in the box.

When working in rows, odd-numbered rows are usually read from right to left and even-numbered rows from left to right.

Odd-numbered rows represent the right side of the work and are usually knit. Even-numbered rows represent the wrong side and are usually purled.

When working in rounds, every row on the chart is a right-side row, and is read from right to left.

Use of Zero

In patterns that include various sizes, zeros are sometimes necessary. For example, k0 (0,1) means if you are making the smallest or middle size, you would do nothing, and if you are making the largest size, you would k1.

Glossary

bind off—used to finish an edge

cast on—process of making foundation stitches used in knitting

decrease—means of reducing the number of stitches in a row

increase—means of adding to the number of stitches in a row

intarsia—method of knitting a multicolored pattern into the fabric

knitwise—insert needle into stitch as if to knit

make 1—method of increasing using the strand between the last stitch worked and the next stitch

place marker—placing a purchased marker or loop of contrasting yarn onto the needle for ease in working a pattern repeat

purlwise—insert needle into stitch as if to purl

right side—side of garment or piece that will be seen when worn

selvage stitch—edge stitch used to make seaming easier

slip, slip, knit—method of decreasing by moving stitches from left needle to right needle and working them together

slip stitch—an unworked stitch slipped from left needle to right needle usually as to purl

wrong side—side that will be inside when garment is worn

work even—continue to work in the pattern as established without working any increases or decreases

work in pattern as established—continue to work following the pattern stitch as it has been set up or established on the needle, working any increases or decreases in such a way that the established pattern remains the same

yarn over—method of increasing by wrapping the yarn over the right needle without working a stitch

TWISTED CORD

To form the cord, hold the number of cords indicated together matching ends. Attach one end to a door knob or hook. Insert a pencil into the opposite end and twist in one direction until the length is tightly twisted and begins to kink.

Once the cord is tightly twisted, continue to hold the twisted end while folding the yarn in the middle. Remove the end from the knob or hook and match the two ends, then release them allowing the cord to twist on itself.

Trim the cord ends to the desired length and knot each end. If the cord is woven through eyelets, it may be necessary to tie a second knot in the end to prevent it from slipping back through the eyelet opening.

FRINGE

Cut a piece of cardboard half as long as specified in instructions for strands plus ½ inch for trimming. Wind yarn loosely and evenly around cardboard. When cardboard is filled, cut yarn across one end. Do this several times then begin fringing. Wind additional strands as necessary.

Single Knot Fringe
Hold specified number of strands for one knot together, fold in half. Hold project to be fringed with right side facing you. Use crochet hook to draw folded end through space or stitch indicated from right to wrong side.

Pull loose ends through folded section.

Draw knot up firmly. Space knots as indicated in pattern instructions.

Double Knot Fringe
Begin by working Single Knot Fringe completely across one end of piece. With right side facing you and working from left to right, take half the strands of one knot and half the strands of the knot next to it and knot them together.

Triple Knot Fringe
Work Double Knot Fringe across. On the right side, work from left to right tying a third row of knots.

Spaghetti Fringe
Following Single Knot Fringe instructions, tie each knot with just one strand of yarn.

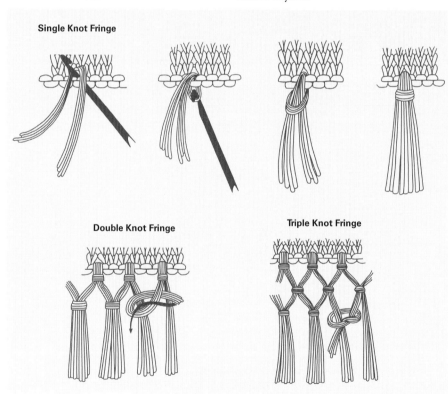

Single Knot Fringe

Double Knot Fringe

Triple Knot Fringe

ABBREVIATIONS & SYMBOLS

[ ] work instructions within brackets as many times as directed

( ) work instructions within parentheses in the place directed

* repeat instructions following the single asterisk as directed

** repeat instructions following the asterisks as directed

" inch(es)

approx approximately

beg begin/beginning

CC contrasting color

ch chain stitch

cm centimeter(s)

cn cable needle

dec decrease/decreases/decreasing

dpn(s) double-pointed needle(s)

g gram

inc increase/increases/increasing

k knit

k2tog knit 2 stitches together

LH left hand

lp(s) loop(s)

m meter(s)

M1 make one stitch

MC main color

mm millimeter(s)

oz ounce(s)

p purl

pat(s) pattern(s)

p2tog purl 2 stitches together

psso pass slipped stitch over

rem remain/remaining

rep repeat(s)

rev St st reverse stockinette stitch

RH right hand

rnd(s) rounds

RS right side

skp slip, knit, pass stitch over—one stitch decreased

sk2p slip 1, knit 2 together, pass slip stitch over the knit 2 together; 2 stitches have been decreased

sl slip

sl 1k slip 1 knitwise

sl 1p slip 1 purlwise

sl st slip stitch(es)

ssk slip, slip, knit these 2 stitches together—a decrease

st(s) stitch(es)

St st stockinette stitch/ stocking stitch

tbl through back loop(s)

tog together

WS wrong side

wyib with yarn in back

wyif with yarn in front

yd(s) yard(s)

yfwd yarn forward

yo yarn over

KNITTING NEEDLES CONVERSION CHART

U.S.	0	1	2	3	4	5	6	7	8	9	10	10½	11	13	15
Metric(mm)	2	2¼	2¾	3¼	3½	3¾	4	4½	5	5½	6	6½	8	9	10

GAUGE

A correct stitch gauge is very important. Please take the time to work a stitch gauge swatch about 4 x 4 inches. Measure the swatch. If the number of stitches and rows are fewer than indicated under "Gauge" in the pattern, your hook is too large. Try another swatch with a smaller size hook. If the number of stitches and rows are more than indicated under "Gauge" in the pattern, your hook is too small. Try another swatch with a larger size hook.

Skill Levels

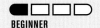

BEGINNER

Projects for first-time knitters using basic knit and purl stitches. Minimal shaping.

EASY

Projects using basic stitches, repetitive stitch patterns, simple color changes and simple shaping and finishing.

INTERMEDIATE

Projects with a variety of stitches, such as basic cables and lace, simple intarsia, double-pointed needles and knitting in the round needle techniques, mid-level shaping and finishing.

EXPERIENCED

Projects using advanced techniques and stitches, such as short rows, Fair Isle, more intricate intarsia, cables, lace patterns and numerous color changes.

Standard Yarn Weight System

Categories of yarn, gauge ranges, and recommended needle sizes

Yarn Weight Symbol & Category Names	1 SUPER FINE	2 FINE	3 LIGHT	4 MEDIUM	5 BULKY	6 SUPER BULKY
Type of Yarns in Category	Sock, Fingering, Baby	Sport, Baby	DK, Light Worsted	Worsted, Afghan, Aran	Chunky, Craft, Rug	Bulky, Roving
Knit Gauge* Ranges in Stockinette Stitch to 4 inches	21–32 sts	23–26 sts	21–24 sts	16–20 sts	12–15 sts	6–11 sts
Recommended Needle in Metric Size Range	2.25–3.25mm	3.25–3.75mm	3.75–4.5mm	4.5–5.5mm	5.5–8mm	8mm
Recommended Needle U.S. Size Range	1 to 3	3 to 5	5 to 7	7 to 9	9 to 11	11 and larger

* GUIDELINES ONLY: The above reflect the most commonly used gauges and needle sizes for specific yarn categories.

American School of Needlework, Berne, IN 46711 • ASNpub.com

HOW TO CROCHET

Some knit items are finished with a crochet trim or edging. Below are some abbreviations used in crochet and a review of some basic crochet stitches.

Crochet Abbreviations

ch	chain stitch
dc	double crochet
hdc	half double crochet
lp(s)	loop(s)
reverse sc	reverse single crochet
sc	single crochet
sl st	slip stitch
yo	yarn over

Chain Stitch (ch)

Begin by making a slip knot on the hook. Bring the yarn over the hook from back to front and draw through the loop on the hook.

For each additional chain stitch, bring the yarn over the hook from back to front and draw through the loop on the hook.

Single Crochet (sc)

Insert the hook in the second chain through the center of the V. Bring the yarn over the hook from back to front.

Draw the yarn through the chain stitch and onto the hook.

Again bring yarn over the hook from back to front and draw it through both loops on hook.

For additional rows of single crochet, insert the hook under both loops of the previous stitch instead of through the

center of the V as when working into the chain stitch.

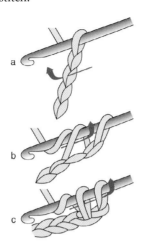

Reverse Single Crochet (rev sc)

Working from left to right, insert hook under both loops of the next stitch to the right.

Bring yarn over hook from back to front and draw through both loops on hook.

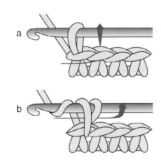

Half-Double Crochet (hdc)

Bring yarn over hook from back to front, insert hook in indicated chain stitch.

Draw yarn through the chain stitch and onto the hook.

Bring yarn over the hook from back to front and draw it through all three loops on the hook in one motion.

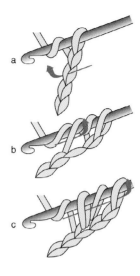

Slip Stitch (sl st)

Insert hook under both loops of the stitch, bring yarn over the hook from back to front and draw it through the stitch and the loop on the hook.

Picot

Picots can be made in a variety of ways so refer to pattern for specific instructions.

Chain required number of stitches. Insert hook at base of chain stitches and through back loop of stitch, complete as indicated in pattern.

DRG Publishing
306 East Parr Road
Berne, IN 46711
©2005 American School of Needlework
TOLL-FREE ORDER LINE or to request a free catalog (800) 582-6643
Customer Service (800) 282-6643, **Fax** (800) 882-6643

Visit AnniesAttic.com.